VOL: I

I0143272

BE A MAN
THE WORLD NEEDS

NATHAN KING

Be a Man the World Needs: Volume One

Copyright © 2024, Nathan King

Published by NK Solutions, LLC.

ISBN: 979-8-9898327-2-9

eBook: 979-8-9898327-3-6

For Clinton King.
Dad, you showed me what it means to
be a man the world needs.

*"My prayer is that when I die,
all of hell rejoices that I
am out of the fight."*
C.S. Lewis

INTRODUCTION

CLIMB THE MOUNTAIN

We were cutting a trail somewhere around 4,000 feet of elevation. Even at that height the air was thick with humidity as a tropical storm smothered the jungle like bush adorning the mountainside. The red clay stuck to our boots. Our gear grew heavier with every cascading drop. It was an adventure. Thankfully, we were on our way down the mountain.

What compelled a group of men to walk a mountain path through the jungle in the middle of the rain during hurricane season?

Men like adventure, but that wasn't the real reason. We also like being invited to try difficult things. We like to test ourselves. Neither of those were the goal of our mountaintop trek.

So why did we go? Why *were* we climbing that particular mountain in that specific spot on that given day in June? Why? Because there was something on top of the mountain worth doing.

We didn't go to see the sights even though we did see some remarkable things. The foliage of banana, plantain, and coffee trees dancing amidst a storm is pretty amazing. Below we glimpsed some of the geography and topography of the roads we had been traveling the previous days. They were laid out like lines on a map. It was a sight to behold. The sliver of blue breaking beyond the tropical front miles away peered like a promise of change through the sky. It was all incredible. It was all secondary. We had climbed the mountain to do something.

At the top of the mountain was a woman and her children. I couldn't name any of them. I had never seen them before. I will never see them again except in the single solitary picture I took of their smiling faces after the work was done. The work is why we climbed the mountain.

What work?

My friends and I had climbed the mountain to make the lives of the lone family on the ridge of the mountain better. We had gone to do something very simple. We were building them a new cooking stove.

In a place where most houses are held together by

mud and sticks, practically all the cooking happens around what most of us would describe as a camp fire. The physical implications on the health of the women and girls who tend these fires is disastrous over time. So we climbed a mountain to improve the quality of life for a woman and her family.

Why? Because that's what men were made for.

THE WORLD'S NEED

There are two really dangerous ideas trying to claw their way to prominence in this world. They are the kind of ideas which always seem to resound across pop culture and the socially conscious. Both are dangerous nonsense.

The first is the notion we don't really need men anymore. Except we all know that is nonsense.

The second dangerous idea is worse. It says that there aren't any real men out there anymore. To put it bluntly—this is a lie puked straight from the pit of hell. There are millions of men out there. Men the world desperately needs. And there are millions of boys waiting for their turn at bat.

What the world doesn't need is another clown beyond a keyboard putting down the real men who bust their butts everyday. They do it to keep our world from falling apart. To keep your world from falling apart. Real men don't need the naysayers to twist the proverbial knife while he plays video games, eats his mom's groceries, and enjoys free rent. What the world doesn't need is more shaming of the elite echelon of actual men who show up everyday to make sure you have water to drink, roads to drive on, and groceries that show up at your local market.

What this world needs is men. Real men. A lot of them. I'm crazy enough to believe they are out there. They don't need your permission. They don't want your applause. They only want to do what they were put here to do.

This world needs men who live on purpose, for a purpose. Men who mean what they say, say what they mean, and aren't afraid to call out the chumps who try to stay somewhere in the middle. The middle is where masculinity goes to die. You either man up or you bow down. You either step up or you stop altogether. I've met hundreds of men who are laying down their lives every day to get it right.

THE MISSION

The original mandate for men has not changed. God spoke to Adam in the Garden and said "be fruitful and multiply". Not because the Garden was a paradise of manicured orchards waiting to be plucked, but because it was a frontier of opportunity.

Adam was to work. He was to strive. He was designed by God to build, grow, and give. It is the essence of the heart of every man. That's what this book is fundamentally about. Getting back to the modus operandi of what it means to be a man.

You are the man the world needs. You are. Believe it. You may not be living like it yet, but you'll get there. You have to. No one else can get there for you. It is 100% on you. There are no shortcuts. The easy road is a dead end. But life is hard. So pick your hard. Or it will run you over. Ready or not, here it comes.

You were designed to make things better. Your strength is sorely needed in this world. And that's putting it lightly. God put something inside you. Allow it to mature into the divinely inspired masculinity available to you. Until you do, there will be something absent in your world.

If you don't live up to what God wants for you, your family will never know what it's like to have a real man in their life. Your daughters will date deadbeats damned to repeat the pattern. Your sons will age into weak boys with beards and bank accounts. And your wife will be lonely—living in a mission half fulfilled.

Believe this. There is an enemy that hates you. He hates everything you are. What are you?

You are the original blueprint for what God

wanted in this world. You are a man. You weren't a backup plan. You were *the* plan.

Yes, we are men the world needs. We all have the potential to be. But we also have the potential to miss the mark big time. Adam did. So do we. But we don't have to live in it.

Your enemy would have you believe you aren't good enough for what God wants in your life. Your enemy is on a mission too. His aim is to steal the blueprint for what God wants to build through your life. He wants to kill the dream God put inside the heart of every man. The bottom line is that your enemy wants to destroy you and everything you stand for. If you take a look at our world, it's hard to say the enemy isn't winning. The enemy won't win. He can't win.

What the world needs right now are men who will step into their place in the fight. Men who will dare to give what it takes, grow into their strength, and build a better world around them. I think you're a man like that. Get ready for the fight of your life.

THE NEED

There's a tremendous difference between what I need and what I want. Most days I want a sixteen ounce steak, loaded mashed potatoes, and a gallon of Dr. Pepper. I learned long ago that eating like that regularly doesn't produce a version of myself I like very much. And, giving in to what I want doesn't shape me into the kind of man the people around me need. What I really need is not what I think I want much of the time.

What I actually want is for the people I love the most to know they can rely on me for the long haul. My life goal is faithfulness. That is my dream. To breathe my last breath at a ripe old age knowing I was faithful to my wife, my children, my family and friends—and the people who depend on me.

This is not a book about what you want. This was written to be a book about what the world needs. The truth is—what the world needs is you! Our world needs men like you to stand up, step up, and man up. We have a role to play. One that is uniquely ours. No one else will do it because no one else can. It belongs to you.

Ironically, whether you've admitted it yet or not, what you actually need is to embrace how much the world needs you. When you do you will step into your place in the big picture. You'll find the spot where your purpose and your God-given passion sync up. It's the one-two-combination that knocks the enemy on his butt. Nothing rattles hell more than a son of God walking in his God-given purpose.

You're not a punk. And you're not a sissy. You *are* a champion of the kingdom of God. His beloved son. Your life carries inherent dignity, value, and purpose on a scale you may have never attempted to consider. Consider it.

The words in these pages aren't meant to be another feckless shot at tearing down men. We are sick of the mud-slinging in our world. We're all tired of the emotional eunuchs parading their image of imposed masculinity on our world. I'm not here to pile it on. I wrote this book because I believe it's time to rally the charge. The only way to stem the tide of limp-hearted cowards telling you what kind of man you're supposed to be is for you to live it so loud they can't help but shy away.

We can't get there by tip-toeing through the issues. We're going to take them head on. What's going to follow is a set of twelve principles. This is designed so you can tackle one per week, per month, or whatever rhythm works. Each entry is short on purpose. I went small on the word count because I'm hoping it will give you the space to go big on reflection. Take the time to think them through. Get around a fire with some dudes and talk them out. At the least, create a text group and challenge one another.

You're a smart guy. So, what you'll notice pretty fast is that some of the maxims presented in this book seem at odds with each other while others seem repetitive. That's not by accident. Some of them will cause tension. That's by design. Step into the tension. Embrace difficulty. The easy path is a dead end. Your people need life. When you walk the hard road you're not being reckless—you're being engaged. You're being honest. You're taking the world as it actually is and you're taking it head on. You're being a man the world needs. Bravo.

CHAPTER 1
BE A MAN THE WORLD NEEDS

"Don't ask what the world needs. Ask what makes you come alive, and go do it. Because what the world needs is people who have come alive."

~ Howard Thurman

1.1 MADE FOR IT

READ: Genesis 1:1-31

> *"And God blessed them. And God said to them, "Be fruitful and multiply and fill the earth and subdue it, and have dominion over the fish of the sea and over the birds of the heavens and over every living thing that moves on the earth." Genesis 1:28 ESV*

God had worked a masterpiece. A world teeming with life and untapped potential. Every syllable of God's creative work set the stage. The blank canvas of possibility was ready.

The world was amazing. It was good. It was new and raw and wild. And it was in need. All that was made was waiting. But for what? The world was lacking one thing. God's amazing creation needed a man. So God made Adam and Eve and called it good. And God gave man stewardship over His creation. God trusted the first man with His creation.

God still trusts men with His creation. You are a man God trusts with His creation. You are a man God trusts with His world.

The first mandate from heaven was to be fruitful and multiply. Because the Garden of Eden wasn't a well-manicured masterpiece of landscaping. It was a landscape of potential, opportunity, and hope.

God still places men where hope is needed. You have everything you need to be a man the world needs. You were created for it.

CHALLENGE: Today, when you encounter a need in your everyday world. Meet it. You may be the only one who can.

1.2 EMBRACE IT

READ: Genesis 37:18-36

"But God sent me ahead of you to preserve for you a remnant on earth and to save your lives by a great deliverance." Genesis 45:7 NIV

Joseph had every reason to play the victim card. He was a real victim. His own brothers had sold him out, literally.

Even in Egyptian slavery, Joseph experienced betrayal, hardship, and loss. But Joseph would not be deterred. Joseph saw the potential on the other side of every difficulty.

Joseph embraced hardship and experienced God's incredible goodness. Ultimately, Joseph's willingness to embrace the moment provided the opportunity to make a profound difference.

When disaster struck, Joseph didn't celebrate the misfortune of his captors. He didn't stomp on the hopes of those who had betrayed, enslaved, and imprisoned him. Joseph once again embraced the need in front of him. Joseph looked for a way to help the world around him. Not only did it save a nation, it saved his family. Joseph didn't look for a way to get back at them, he sought the chance to give himself to an incredible need.

You can spend your life looking for retribution or looking for contribution. A man the world needs will bear the scars of hurt and betrayal. No one gets out of this world alive. But you were made for it. Don't go looking for it, but when hardship comes, don't let it rob you of the opportunity to be a man the world needs. Your friends, family, and neighbors are depending on you.

CHALLENGE: Every day is met with some kind of hardship. Don't ignore it today. Look for the opportunity hiding there. How can you be the man the world needs in this situation?

1.3 STAY CALM

READ: Exodus 14:1-31

"The Lord himself will fight for you. Just stay calm." Exodus 14:14 NLT

Imagine escaping slavery after generations. Suddenly the people of Israel experienced incredible freedom! Only, it seemed short-lived. As they camped at the edge of the sea, the armies of their oppressors bore down on them.

The weight of the terror of it must have been horrible. There stood multitudes of men facing the reality of a situation they knew they were powerless to stop. Their wives, children, families and friends were depending on them.

In that moment what the world needed wasn't for the men of Israel to pick up swords they didn't have and charge into the fray against the Egyptians. What the world needed was for the men of Israel to calm their fears. They had to choose trust in God over the reality of what they saw before them.

Sometimes your world will need you to step into danger. There will be moments to be bold, decisive, and aggressive. There will also be moments when you must simply trust God. Always be ready to act. Also, be ready to trust. Stay calm.

The headlines are full of men who lose their cool. You're not going to be one of them. When trouble comes, you know you were made for it. You're ready to embrace it. You're calm because you know God himself will fight for you.

CHALLENGE: It's going to happen. Something is going to surprise you today. It may push all the right buttons. When it comes, don't lose your cool. Don't panic. Stay calm. Even if it's for just 30 seconds at a time.

1.4 GO TO SERVE

READ: 1 Samuel 17:1-58

"And David said to Saul, "Let no man's heart fail because of him. Your servant will go and fight with this Philistine." 1 Samuel 17:32 ESV

David's father asked him to take his brothers' lunch. But what the world needed was more than someone delivering bread and cheese. Another confrontation waited. Another opportunity.

The story of David and Goliath is the pivotal story of David's life. It propelled him into prominence. The spotlight found David forever after. But he did not go seeking it. David went to serve his father.

David shined when he served. His heart for working on behalf of those around him caused people to love him. Sometimes serving looked like hanging out with the sheep, sometimes it meant facing giants. But it was David's time with the sheep that prepared him for the encounter with Goliath.

The world needs men who are willing to serve in obscurity with a selfless heart. The time with the sheep when no one is looking is a proving ground for the valley where everyone watches. David stepped into the conflict with faith. God had proven himself faithful. The arrogant giant proclaiming himself an enemy of God was another opportunity.

David served his father first. He served his family. He did what was asked and what was required. It created in him the kind of willing heart that made him capable of faithfully confronting the giant.

You are surrounded by giants. They are everywhere. But we must be willing to walk through seasons of preparation in order to experience moments of deliverance. Serving for the sake of serving is often thankless and seemingly overlooked. God sees. God knows. What you do is not forgotten. It is practice for the giants the world needs you to slay.

CHALLENGE: Today, you will encounter an opportunity to do something that seems thankless and insignificant. Do it with an eager heart.

1.5 SEND ME

READ: Nehemiah 2:1-20

"And I said to the king, "If it pleases the king, and if your servant has found favor in your sight, that you send me to Judah, to the city of my fathers' graves, that I may rebuild it." Nehemiah 2:5 ESV

Every day, Nehemiah stood in the presence of the king. He was close, faithful, and always there to serve his king. But the plight of his people weighed on him. Nehemiah saw the world in need but did not merely see it. He decided to do something about it.

The land of his fathers was in chaos. The place of his people. There was a tremendous need, and it gripped his heart. The cupbearer was in a position to make such a big demand of a king. He was a servant. He was the king's property. But the king asked. Nehemiah's faithfulness had created an opportunity for authenticity. When the moment came, Nehemiah didn't balk. He acted.

Nehemiah took his awareness of the world's need to one who could do something about it. And, more importantly, he had a willingness to participate in the solution. Nehemiah wasn't trying to solve someone else's problems by proxy or secondhand. He was willing to go.

What did Nehemiah know about building walls, leading people, or cross-country travel? Nothing. He was a cupbearer. Like many others before and so many after, Nehemiah's willingness to faithfully attend to the need in front of him every day positioned him to do what was next.

Our world is bombarded by voices screaming about what they believe the world needs. It's become so ubiquitous that it has become background noise. The world doesn't need another voice pointing fingers at secondhand problems. The world needs men who are willing to say, "Send me."

CHALLENGE: When you see a problem today, don't just point it out to someone else. Become part of the solution.

DISCUSSION

What does it mean to be a man God trusts with His world?

What does it look like to embrace hardship and see the opportunity in it?

What are some practical ways to stay calm and trust God when facing unexpected challenges?

What small, seemingly insignificant tasks have prepared you for larger challenges in life?

How can we take personal responsibility for addressing the needs we see around us? When did you meet a need?

How can we cultivate a willingness to say, "Send me," when we encounter problems?

Which of these themes do you find most challenging, and why?

How can we hold each other accountable in our journey to becoming men the world needs?

NOTES

_____

_____

_____

_____

_____

_____

_____

_____

_____

_____

_____

_____

_____

_____

_____

_____

_____

_____

_____

_____

_____

_____

CHAPTER 2
BE A MAN OF FAITH

"Great faith is the product of great fights."

~ Smith Wigglesworth

2.1 FIGHT TO BELIEVE

READ: Hebrews 1:1-40

"Now faith is the assurance of things hoped for, the conviction of things not see." Hebrews 11:1 ESV

Faith is not easy—not for everyone. But we all have a little born into us. That's a good thing, too, because our world is brimming with opportunities to put faith into motion.

Every time I turn my key, I believe my car will start. Every time I pull the trigger on my rifle, I have faith the shot fired will help put food on my table. And each night I close my eyes to sleep, I have faith I will wake up able to do it all over again the next day.

We live in a world that is all too often quick to discredit notions of faith. However, the need for faith is daily, constant, and tremendous.

A man with the power to believe is one who fights to keep his faith. This is harder for some than others. But it is essential for men. A man who loses the ability to believe loses hope, trust, and purpose.

Be a man who develops a deep conviction for the things you believe in. The best convictions are born of experience. I have a deep assurance that my wife wants what is best for me. I know this because I have experienced the truth of it firsthand for years. This has made me a man who has faith in her. I believe her actions will benefit me because of our shared history and her track record of doing so.

The world needs men who have a relationship with God centered on experience. Be a man rich in experiencing the goodness of God. The way we experience the goodness of God is to put our faith in Him. We choose to believe. The world is in desperate need of men who will choose to believe, even when it is hard.

CHALLENGE: Doubt is going to hit you today. Choose to believe. It's not easy, but it is simple. You got this.

2.2 WALK THE WALK

READ: Genesis 5:1-32

"Enoch walked faithfully with God; then he was no more, because God took him away." Genesis 5:24 NIV

Imagine claiming to have a deep conviction you say determines your actions. What if you told everyone about it? But then you never did anything about it?

Your world is full of men who say one thing and do something else. You're not one of them. When you say something you do it. Your words aren't empty. Your feet take you where your heart points you. You are a man of faith.

The world needs men who walk the walk. It is real to them. No more carefully curated images. No shiny exteriors covering up a toxic heart. The real thing.

Enoch was a man in scripture who lived it. He was known for it. The cool thing about being a man who actually walks out his faith is that he is a man who walks with God. When you walk out your faith in sincerity and authenticity, you are giving God access to your everyday world–through you.

Imagine a world where your spouse, children,

grandchildren, coworkers, friends, and neighbors have a daily encounter with the goodness of God. It is possible. Even better, it is probable when you are a man living an authentic life of faith in God. That is the kind of man your world needs.

CHALLENGE: Identify one daily habit that does not align with your goals.

2.3 FORWARD FAITH

READ: Genesis 17:1-27

"For he was looking forward to the city that has foundations, whose designer and builder is God."
Hebrews 11:10 ESV

What do you have to look forward to? I hope it's something great. When you have something to look forward to it creates an underlying sense of purpose in your life. Anticipation is powerful.

I anticipate that my children have great things ahead of them in life. I anticipate that my wife and I still have many wonderful years ahead of us to experience together. I anticipate God will lead me into many more opportunities to help people and proclaim his goodness.

Anticipation comes in two forms. You can eagerly embrace what is next. Or, you can toil with a sense of dread. No matter which posture you choose to embrace there is a common truth—life is hard.

The man who eagerly embraces the opportunity in front of him is the one who continues to encounter another incredible opportunity. He is a man of faith. Those who default to a victim mindset bemoan their past so much that they undermine their future. They castrate their own faith before there is even a chance of conception.

Be a man of faith. Be a man who wakes up ready to face another day. Be a man who longs for the next one —even as he eagerly embraces the toil of the day.

CHALLENGE: Don't complain about anything today. When you see a challenge instead proclaim the opportunity it presents for God to show you His faithfulness to you.

2.4 CONSIDER WELL

READ: Exodus 3:1-22

"He considered the reproach of Christ greater wealth than the treasures of Egypt, for he was looking to the reward." Hebrews 11:26 ESV

Some days, I feel like all I do is make decisions all day long. These days, we even have a term for the psychological effect it has on us. It is called decision fatigue. I know there are seasons when it seems like I am daily laboring under the effects of decision fatigue.

Decisions are before you today. When we're tired, fed up, or angry it becomes even more difficult to make the right decision. Compounding all of this is the nature of the wrongness we see and experience as part of our everyday world.

Godlessness and sin are rampant. But you and I are not surprised by that. This world has been suffering the wages of sin since the failure of Adam. Perhaps he should have taken a little more time to consider his options.

Jesus is the man the world needed to overcome the sin Adam's failings brought upon all of us. Similarly, you are the man your world needs to counter the effects of the evil schemes around you. Consider well.

How will your decisions impact those who depend on you? Don't fall into the habits and patterns of the chaos around you. Don't embrace the identity the broken world thrusts upon you. Know this. You are a man the world needs. You were born into it. As a man of faith you can stop to consider your options and step toward the one that honors God and blesses your world.

CHALLENGE: Avoid any knee-jerk reactions to decision-making today. Trust your instincts as a son of God. But also take some time to evaluate how your decision will honor God and bless people around you.

2.5 ONE MORE TIME

READ: Joshua 6:1-27

"By faith the walls of Jericho fell down after they had been encircled for seven days." Hebrews 11:30 ESV

Joshua and his peers had the benefit of knowing the number of times they were going to march around the city of Jericho. They obeyed God and they believed God. They put their faith into action.

In our quick fix kind of culture doing anything consistently while hoping for a desired outcome seems crazy. It is certainly countercultural. I've heard this statement many times, "hope is not a plan of action." This sentiment is completely true.

Hope without action is lazy. Belief without work is empty. The world doesn't need another man whose head and heart are full of well-wishes and pie in the sky sentiments. What your world does need is a man willing to believe in the amazing things God desires to do around you. What your world needs is a man who proves his belief by getting to work.

What wall stands before you? Perhaps God placed you at this place and time to be the one to bring the wall down. All you have to do is begin to circle it in faith. Put your faith into motion. Don't just wish it will fall, take one more step as you circle it. With every step expect the wall to come down. How many times should you march around the walls in your life? If it's still standing, one more time.

CHALLENGE: What is the wall in your world that needs to come down? This may take some time to consider. Or, you may know right away. Begin to believe and act as if the wall is coming down. Prepare yourself.

DISCUSSION

How do you define faith? Share a specific instance where your faith was tested. How can past experiences strengthen you for the future?

How can you ensure that your actions consistently align with your professed beliefs?

How does having something to look forward to influence your daily life and faith journey?

Can you share an example of a time when anticipation of a positive outcome helped you stay motivated and faithful?

What role does reflection and consideration play in your daily decision-making process? How do you handle decision fatigue?

How do you stay motivated to keep taking steps of faith, even when the outcome isn't immediately visible?

Which theme discussed in this chapter do you find most challenging, and why?

NOTES

_____

_____

_____

_____

_____

_____

_____

_____

_____

_____

_____

_____

_____

_____

_____

_____

_____

_____

_____

_____

_____

CHAPTER 3
BE A MAN OF INFLUENCE

"Leadership is influence."

~ John Maxwell

3.1 RULE OVER IT

READ: Genesis 4:1-26

> *If you do what is right, will you not be accepted?*
> *But if you do not do what is right, sin is crouching*
> *at your door; it desires to have you, but you must*
> *rule over it." Genesis 4:7 NIV*

The hardest person to lead is the one in your mirror. I don't know about you, but I can talk myself into anything. Sometimes I even talk myself into good things. The world needs men capable of ruling over their impulses.

Every one of us has battles to fight, inside and outside. I'll be the first one to line up and tell you how tired I am of constantly listening to the Church berate men. I am equally tired of a Church that fails to properly challenge us as men. The world needs you!

Your relationship with God is not defined by "sin management." Trying to boil it down to that is a tragic misrepresentation of your relationship with God. But we can't gloss it over either.

As a man you are going to routinely encounter temptation. It is going to happen every day. And, you don't have to be the kind of guy who gives in to it. You are a son of God. You have within you, the ability to rule over it.

Imagine a world where kids see their fathers daily shrugging off the attempted advances of sin. As a son of God you were reborn into a kingdom of authority. You have authority over the darker impulses that long to trip you up. You must rule over it. Your world needs you to.

CHALLENGE: When temptation hits you today, declare this simple statement, "You're not my boss.

3.2 LIVE WITH INTEGRITY

READ: Daniel 6:1-28

> *"At this, the administrators and the satraps tried to find grounds for charges against Daniel in his conduct of government affairs, but they were unable to do so. They could find no corruption in him, because he was trustworthy and neither corrupt nor negligent." Daniel 6:4 NIV*

The weight of your integrity is your influence. It is the ability you possess to alter, change, and add value to the happenings around you through relationships. Whether you want influence or not, you have it.

Your ability to lead yourself well is the foundation of influence worth having. Plenty of men have significant amounts of influence, but they have no integrity. They aren't men of character. Their conduct is not shaped by living as a son of God.

Your influence starts with your integrity. Just as your faith is fashioned by daily trusting God, your influence is strengthened by integrity. Your reputation enhances your influence. This isn't about downplaying your foibles or sweeping your faults under the rug. Integrity is about actually living the life you portray in the public arena.

Your character and integrity are the light of your soul. There is a brightness to it that invades the darkness of this world. There is a weight to it that is unavoidable. Your world needs a man with influence worth following.

CHALLENGE: Spend a few minutes making a list of the values you live by that demonstrate your integrity. Write them down. When faced with a difficult decision, look at your list.

3.3 WHAT YOU CAN

READ: Numbers 13:1-33

But Caleb tried to quiet the people as they stood before Moses. "Let's go at once to take the land," he said. "We can certainly conquer it!" Numbers 13:30 NLT

The time will come when you will be chosen. They will pick you to represent them. Maybe you'll be on a committee. Perhaps you'll be appointed to solve a problem. It could be that someone will ask you to participate in a cadre of leaders. There are many forms this request could take. But it happens to every man of influence. Your reputation will cause others to seek your aid.

As you tread the difficult path of leadership and influence you are walking exactly where you have been commissioned by God to go. He sent you there, ahead of the others, on behalf of your world. It takes a bold and courageous man of influence to go out as a pathfinder on behalf of his people.

Walk the paths. See the landscape. Take stock of the situation. And when you come back to those who asked for your help, speak the truth. Speak your heart and your mind. Do it with grit and determination. Do everything you know how to do to share what you've learned.

A man of influence knows there are limits. You bear the responsibility for stating your case. Your responsibility carries a burden to do it well. Understand that it may not be enough.

People are going to disagree with you. People are going to hate and resent you. Especially the cowardly and the insecure. Nothing makes those who are already afraid more afraid than someone who is not afraid. Your world can't afford for you to live afraid. And, it can't afford for you to remain quiet. Influence what you can.

CHALLENGE: Speak the truth today when given the opportunity. Do it with bold and compassionate kindness. Someone won't like it, but that doesn't mean they don't need to hear it.

3.4 YOUR NAME

READ: Genesis 41:1-57

> *"A good name is more desirable than great riches;*
> *to be esteemed is better than silver or gold."*
> *Proverbs 22:1 NIV*

We live in the age of personal branding. The "creator economy" is rampant online. People peddle their names alongside ideas and intangibles to turn a quick buck. There is nothing wrong with making money. There is nothing wrong with being creative and using your platform to better your financial reality. There is a lot wrong with cheapening your name in pursuit of a dollar.

Probably most of your clothes have a name on them. Your car and even the person who designed your house bear a name. Names mean something. People will pay a premium for a name. How valuable is your name?

I think about my name a lot. My family has passed down a great name to me. It carries significance. When I think about my name I think about the values I was raised on. Things like working hard, loving God, living with integrity, and caring for my family. I want those values to mean something to my children.

In order for my name to mean something my actions must reflect the values I want to be remembered for. If I want to be remembered as honest I must not be dishonest. Your name carries your influence.

In our culture many people carry incredible influence for almost no reason. Sometimes they are getting by on the fickle attention of the mob. Sometimes they are living off the borrowed influence of those who came before. Maybe they had a rich grandparent or parent and were able to inherit their influence to a large measure. That can only last for so long. Eventually your actions must match your esteem. Be mindful of your esteem.

The world needs men who live the reputation going before them. Your world is in need of a man who carries a good name. A good name is esteemed. Eagerness precedes the arrival of a good name. When you carry a good name your world will long for you to show up.

CHALLENGE: Ask a friend or colleague to write a short simple list of the values and attributes they think of when they hear your name. Compare it to the list you made in the previous section. Does it match?

3.5 COMPOUND INTEREST

READ: Luke 16:1-31

> *"Whoever can be trusted with very little can also be trusted with much, and whoever is dishonest with very little will also be dishonest with much."*
> *Luke 16:10 NIV*

You will be trusted with simple things at first. People trust you with relationships. They trust you with responsibilities. It stacks up.

The way we handle our opportunities says a lot about us. A man who takes a small trust and protects it becomes worthy of larger trust. As your ability to be trusted grows and flourishes so will your opportunities.

Your reputation will flourish based on your faithfulness. Your influence will skyrocket, or it will plummet, based on your track record. Small faithfulness leads to small influence. Incredible faithfulness proves incredible trustworthiness, leading to tremendous influence.

Who would willingly choose to have no influence? Especially with those most important to them. Not you. You are a man who wants to influence his world. And your world needs your influence. Your world needs your ability to step into a given situation and leverage your God-given abilities for improvement.

How you manage the small things speaks volumes about you. Pay your bills on time. Be honest. Do what you say. Take care of your property. Work hard. As your faithfulness grows your opportunities grow. Demonstrating faithfulness opens doors in your life.

If this is something you've struggled with in the past it's not too late. The beautiful thing about faithfulness is that it is so much like compound interest. Invest a little now and just keep at it, it will grow over time.

Something truly wonderful happens to a man who continuously proves to be faithful in all the small things. He doesn't just encounter bigger and better opportunities. He grows into the kind of man worth being trusted with incredible opportunities. The world needs more men like that.

CHALLENGE: What is one thing you can do today that perhaps no one else around you can do? Do it. Do it well. Do it for days to come. Do it again, and again, and again to demonstrate your faithfulness.

DISCUSSION

How important is it for children to see their fathers resisting temptation? What are some specific strategies you use to resist temptation?

Can you share an example of a recent temptation you faced that you were able to overcome? How can we exercise authority over our impulses?

What does it mean to live with integrity? How does this affect your influence on others? Can you give an example from your own experience?

How do you ensure that your public portrayal matches your private actions?

What steps can you take to live courageously and not let fear dictate your actions?

How do you build and maintain a good name? Share some values or principles that guide you.

How have you demonstrated trustworthiness in small things, and how has this led to greater responsibilities and opportunities?

NOTES

_____
_____
_____
_____
_____
_____
_____
_____
_____
_____
_____
_____
_____
_____
_____
_____
_____
_____
_____
_____
_____
_____

CHAPTER 4
BE A MAN THAT IS CAPABLE

"If you are afraid to fail, you will never do the things you are capable of doing."

~ John Wooden

4.1 FOLLOW ME

READ: Matthew 4:1-25

"Follow my example, as I follow the example of Christ." 1 Corinthians 11:1 NIV

Remember the classic Arnold line from the Terminator? No, not "I'll be back." I'm talking about "come with me if you want to live." It was always a bit melodramatic but that was the point. The world needs a man worth following.

The pinnacle man to follow was Jesus. But you can be a man following Jesus whom others follow. It's not complicated. Love people the way Jesus did. Love your neighbor. Add value to this world by giving your best.

The world needs another man worth following. Obviously you're never going to be perfect. Perfection isn't the goal. Making the world around you better is.

Your sons need you to look them in the eyes and say, "follow me." Do it with your words, your actions, and your life. Leverage your integrity and your unique place in this world to be a man others follow.

Are you qualified? Are you capable of being someone others follow? You are, but you may not realize it yet. Maybe there's a voice in your head constantly calling your qualifications into doubt.

Ignore the voices like that. If you're following Jesus with your life you are worth following. His qualifications have been lent to you.

What do we do with that? We acknowledge the grace in our lives and do our part to grow in our capacity. Continue to mature in wisdom, faith, and leadership. Someone in your world needs to follow you as you follow Jesus.

CHALLENGE: What are you the most capable of doing? Leverage that ability today in a way that points someone toward Jesus.

4.2 USE IT

READ: Exodus 28:1-43

> *"Instruct all the skilled craftsmen whom I have filled with the spirit of wisdom. Have them make garments for Aaron that will distinguish him as a priest set apart for my service." Exodus 28:3*

I don't care who you are, you were born with the ability to do something incredible. Each of us are. It could be a high capacity for engineering, math, art or mountaineering. You have inside you (already) the disposition to be good at something. Grow in it, and then use your God-given skill.

We all have abilities to do things. Some are things we learn and train for. Some are things we seem naturally good at. Take what you are naturally good at, and work to get even better. Train, learn, and excel to incredible levels. And, use your skill to glorify God. Use your skill to help the people around you. You were given skill so you can bless the world.

Operate in wisdom. A capable man takes what he is good at and sees how to apply it. Our world is in need of men with the discretion to leverage their talents in critical situations. We needed it yesterday. Your kids need it.

Someone has to set an example. Continue to dig deep into your heart. Rediscover the man God has made you to be. Realize your potential. Your capacity is a gift to the world. Steward your ability. Grow in it. And then unleash it on a world desperately in need of your ability.

CHALLENGE: What are you good at? Do something with it today to help someone. Do something tomorrow to get even better at it. Never stop growing.

4.3 ACT LIKE IT

READ: 1 Kings 2:1-46

> *"I am about to go the way of all the earth," he said.*
> *"So be strong, act like a man." 1 Kings 2:2 NIV*

The conduct of men is under direct fire in our life-time. It's happening to young boys in the school system and sometimes even our churches. Increasingly, culture seems designed to try and curb the instincts of boys until they act more like girls.

The tragedy of this has been creeping up on us for decades. In our lifetime the bill has come due. Skilled tradesmen and craftsmen are all but vanishing. Men of moral authority, integrity, and backbone seem few and far between. Those committed and capable are like diamonds in the ruff.

People gravitate toward the things in their world that are celebrated. Here's a hard truth. Not very many people are going to celebrate someone who acts like a real man. In fact, they are going to resent it. Because a real man makes them uncomfortable. The insecure fickle masses cringe in the looming shadow of mascu-line ability. There is a good reason for this. Men have done horrible things, but that's not an excuse to castrate a society. We don't need an effeminate culture. We need real men, acting like real men.

You are a man. Act like it. Our world is inundated with broken notions of virtue bent on false appearances. Forget that. Do an incredible job of loving, leading, and serving the people immediately around you. A man is someone who is tough, capable, and fierce. Be fierce in your loyalty, love, and grit.

Be able and be capable. Act like a man. Go to work. Discipline your life. Love those around you. Don't back down from a fight worth having. Do go above and beyond to show tenderness and compassion. The world needs capable men.

CHALLENGE: Let your words reflect your strength today. Speak with conviction. Tell the people you love what they mean to you. Take a stand for the truth.

4.4 STRONG COURAGE

READ: Joshua 1:1-18

> *"Have I not commanded you? Be strong and coura-*
> *geous. Do not be frightened, and do not be*
> *dismayed, for the Lord your God is with you wher-*
> *ever you go." Joshua 1:9 ESV*

Your ability to accomplish is a defining trait of your masculinity. It's a design feature. God made men capable. Even so, the capable man will come up short without the courage to step into the arena.

What you are able to do is irrelevant if you're too afraid to try. Fear has to be punched in the face every day. Fear never goes away on its own. Courage is something you will have to learn to grab hold of. You weren't born to be timid.

Becoming capable is a major part of becoming the kind of man your world needs. Boyhood is precisely about growing into that kind of man. Courage is equally important. The truth is, if you have the prowess to accomplish a feat, but do not have the courage then you are incapable.

Don't be another talented, brilliant coward. Or even worse, don't be one of the sad sacks too busy hiding from the real world and all its problems. Have the courage to make the attempt. As you find the courage to keep trying, you will grow until you gain the strength to succeed. Your world needs you to succeed.

CHALLENGE: What is something you've been too afraid to do? Take a step toward doing it today. Even if it's a small step. Go for it. Do it again tomorrow.

4.5 GOD GIVES

READ: Exodus 31:1-18

"and I have filled him with the Spirit of God, with wisdom, with understanding, with knowledge and with all kinds of skills..." Exodus 31:3 NIV

Your ability is a gift. God has given it to you. But it wasn't given to you so you could hide it in your heart. You were not blessed with your ability so you could keep it tucked away for your private benefit. You were meant to unleash your gift upon the world.

The ability God grants to you is a holy thing. It is a result of the Holy Spirit himself at work inside of you. God doesn't do things halfway. He fills you up with it. Perhaps that is why when men encounter their gift they seem to become obsessed with it.

Aim your holy obsession at the things this world needs from you. Go at it with gusto. Leverage what God has given you in order to make the world a better place. Your capacity to do this is so far beyond what you realize. As you leverage your God-given gift it will grow.

When you live out your capability in front of the world, the world will tell you how needed you are. Often it will be very clear, like someone directly asking you, or a clear need you encounter. However, it may not always be overt. There may seem to be some ambiguity to it. This is when you will need to wade into the situation with a tremendous amount of wisdom as well.

You are a man the world needs. You are a man who is capable. God has given you the capability to make a tremendous difference. With that ability comes an incredible purpose. God gives us a purpose and He gives us the means to fulfill that purpose. Your purpose will involve improving the world around you. How will you choose to use your God-given ability? Pray to be able. Seek to have wisdom. Create, plan, dream, pursue, and make this world better. That's what God wants for you.

CHALLENGE: Take a moment to thank God for His gifts. The Holy Spirit is the difference maker.

DISCUSSION

What does it mean to you to be a man worth following?

How does following Jesus enhance your ability to lead others effectively?

How can you identify and use your God-given abilities to bless those around you? What are some skills or talents you possess that you can use to serve others?

What steps can you take to ensure you are always growing in your capabilities?

What characteristics define a real man in your perspective, and how can you embody them?

How can you balance toughness with tenderness in your interactions with others?

How can you prepare yourself to tackle tough issues with courage and faith?

What fears hold you back from stepping into your full potential as a man?

NOTES

_____

_____

_____

_____

_____

_____

_____

_____

_____

_____

_____

_____

_____

_____

_____

_____

_____

_____

_____

_____

CHAPTER 5
BE A MAN ON PURPOSE

"Act as if what you do makes a difference. It does."

~ William James

5.1 CONSIDER YOUR WAYS

READ: Haggai 1:1-15

Now, therefore, thus says the Lord of hosts: Consider your ways. Haggai 1:5 ESV

You only get to live one life in this world. Your resources are important. Especially your time. It would be a shame to waste your life.

Tragically, this is exactly what you and I encounter daily. Our world is full of those who have chosen to pursue pleasure over purpose. They fill their days with empty busyness. Hobbies, addictions, selfishness, and other distractions dominate their time.

Every life was meant to be filled with purpose. You can't be your own purpose. You can't fulfill or satisfy yourself. You can't cover up your own shortcomings by just trying to work harder.

However, you can discover true purpose, contentment, and forgiveness. This kind of purpose is found in God alone. Living in pursuit of what God wants for you and your world will put you on the path to purpose.

Every man needs a holy moment when he is forced to reflect on his purpose. In this moment we reflect on our days and what fills them. No man can answer those questions for another. But we can help and guide each other. As you strive to be a man the world needs, you will tread the path of purpose. How could you expect to live any other way?

Take some time today to evaluate your pursuits. It's time to get really honest about how you spend your time, effort, and resources. Are you building a life of pleasure or a life or purpose?

Consider your ways. Some bad things need to go. Kick them out of your life. Some good things are taking up too much of your time. Don't cut them out, pair them back. Replace them with the great things God wants to aim you at. Consider the path before you and make a choice.

CHALLENGE: Evaluate your daily habits and routines. Make a list. Beside each entry write if the habit is bad, good, or great. Use this list to determine how you'll try to adjust moving forward.

5.2 SEE IT

READ: Proverbs 29:1-29

If people can't see what God is doing, they stumble all over themselves; But when they attend to what he reveals, they are most blessed. Proverbs 29:18 MSG

Do you have the capacity to see ahead with optimism? I'm not talking about pie-in-the-sky wishful thinking. As men, we must be able to look at a situation and discern a path that leads to a better outcome.

We were designed to add value to our world. You were made to navigate the circumstances of your unique situation. But we will never be able to do it if we are inattentive.

Purpose requires attention. Purpose requires intention. Living your purpose will demand something from you. It will demand everything. That begins with your willingness to pay attention.

Many men ignore the realities of their circumstances. They don't engage their children. Their wives are left to wallow in an emotionally hollow existence. They "quiet quit" on their career just to draw a paycheck from a job that offers no pursuit of meaning.

Your purpose is not going to punch you in the face

and say, "Hey! Here I am!" You have to wake up and look for it. Pay attention to what God wants to do in your everyday world.

Too many guys are waiting for some miraculous event where God points at the horizon and says something like, "You'll encounter the mission you've been waiting for over there." This is the exception, not the rule.

A man who is striving to live on purpose pays attention to the world around him. Right where he is. Stop yearning for the next big thing. Stop chasing the horizon. Set about making your world a better place right where you are.

God's purpose for you doesn't always come with a set of GPS coordinates. *X* marks the spot right where you are. The world needs you to pay attention, get busy, and see what God wants to do through your life.

CHALLENGE: Take out the list from yesterday's challenge. Which habit has the potential for the largest positive impact on your family? Consider how you can begin to improve and grow in this area of your life.

5.3 MAKE PLANS

READ: Proverbs 16:1-33

> *"The heart of man plans his way, but the Lord establishes his steps." Proverbs 16:9 ESV*

I loved the A-Team growing up. Do you recall the classic line from Hannibal? He said, "I love it when a plan comes together."

Each of us have a different level of skill when it comes to planning. Some guys seem to make planning easy. For some of us, planning is a little more difficult. There are men who can peer ahead into the future and a vision for what to do almost seems to reveal itself.

There is an unavoidable truth when it comes to living as a man on purpose. It will not happen by accident. You have to embrace it. You have to plan for it.

Planning for some purposes may seem easier than others. If not easy, then perhaps more straightforward. If your purpose is to establish a new nonprofit organization or build something, that kind of planning comes with well established processes you can follow. Some purposes require a different kind of plan.

A man who wants to grow old and stay in love with his wife must plan for it. The man who wants his children to desire his company in their adult years must plan for it. The one who desires to always encounter meaningful work has to plan for it.

These kinds of plans require just as much intentionality as external blueprints and organizational mission statements. Plans like these are called habits. The man living on purpose determines his habits. He's not a slave to his whims. He puts in the work to become a product of good habits. Your habits are the plan you have made for your decisions and behaviors. Build habits that will help you plan for your purpose.

CHALLENGE: Take out your list from the last couple of days. Is there something on the list you labeled as great, but hasn't received enough attention or time? Consider what kind of habit you could begin to build to take steps in that direction. Don't over complicate it. Make it easy. Take it one day at a time.

5.4 NO ACCIDENTS

READ: Genesis 6:1-22

> *"Noah did this; he did all that God commanded him." Genesis 6:22 ESV*

Noah didn't build the ark by accident. He discovered his purpose. There was a plan. There was a season to prepare. Then he faithfully executed the plan.

The ark didn't go up overnight. He didn't lay out the boards, wake up the next morning, and find a giant wooden ship longer than three football fields standing ready to be boarded. Noah labored over the ark daily. It took him decades.

Do you think he did it alone? Of course not. His family helped him. In Noah's journey to fulfill his mission he commissioned his children to participate. By watching Noah live as a man on purpose his sons got a front row seat to discovering God's purpose in their own lives.

Embracing what you were designed to do means doing it with intent. It requires an internal acknowledgement joined with external effort. Purpose requires effort.

The man of faith understands he has been made capable. He has grown into it. He knows his purpose is what the world needs from him. He stands ready. You stand ready.

Rescue never happens by accident. Intervention is not happenstance. The dire circumstances of the day will not be circumvented. They can only be countered. Someone has to be willing to follow the plan that will lead to rescue. A hammer never swings itself.

Pick up your hammer. See hope where no else dares to. Lead with the influence God has given you. Embrace the plan. Execute. Be a man who does it on purpose.

CHALLENGE: Embrace today fully. Whatever is on your list of things to get done, go at them on purpose. Bring the full measure of your intentionality to each given moment.

5.5 WHAT IT IS FOR

READ: Judges 7:1-25

> *The three companies blew the trumpets and smashed the jars. Grasping the torches in their left hands and holding in their right hands the trumpets they were to blow, they shouted, "A sword for the Lord and for Gideon!" Judges 7:20 NIV*

There is a reason why you were born where you were born. There is a reason why you live where you live. Your life has a purpose and a meaning. God wanted you there. You were born into an incredible opportunity. As your influence and faith grows so too does your capacity.

Few men start the journey to God-given masculinity itching for conflict. The truth is we should desire holy conflict. We should long for the opportunity to be used by God to set things right.

That doesn't mean we should go around looking for an opportunity to punch bad guys in the face like something from a comic book. It does mean we refuse to shy away from our strength when the need arises.

You and I both know that need is everywhere around us. Your world needs your strength. Your world needs you to stand up. Take stock of your situation.

Don't hide behind your responsibilities. See the larger responsibility unveiled in the trouble before you.

As you embrace your God-given capacity to tackle the tough stuff in your world, realize what it is for. Who else is going to solve the difficult problems of the day? It certainly won't be selfish people bent on pursuing selfish desires. It won't be those cowardly souls who abuse their positions of authority.

The man who has embraced his capacity understands the purpose for that capacity. It was given to you for a reason. You are capable because God wants you to be capable. God wants you to use your capacity to help His world. God wants you to do it on purpose.

CHALLENGE: Draw a sword on a slip of paper and put it somewhere you will see while you work. Every time you encounter something difficult, look at the sword. Remember, what you're doing it for.

DISCUSSION

What does it mean to you to live with purpose, mission, and intentionality in your daily life?

What are some common distractions that can lead us away from living with purpose? How can we overcome them?

How does having a clear vision of God's purpose for your life help you stay focused?

What is one practical step you can take to embrace your God-given purpose?

How do you balance planning for the future with trusting God to establish your steps?

What habits can you cultivate to help you stay on track with your purpose and goals?

What role does perseverance play in fulfilling your purpose?

How can you involve others in your purpose?

NOTES

_____

_____

_____

_____

_____

_____

_____

_____

_____

_____

_____

_____

_____

_____

_____

_____

_____

_____

_____

_____

CHAPTER 6
BE A MAN WHO DOES HARD THINGS

"The impediment to action advances action. What stands in the way becomes the way."

~ Marcus Aurelius

6.1 HOLD ON

READ: 2 Samuel 23:1-39

> *"...but Eleazar stood his ground and struck down the Philistines till his hand grew tired and froze to the sword. The Lord brought about a great victory that day. The troops returned to Eleazar, but only to strip the dead." 2 Samuel 23:10 NIV*

Technology and advancement often seem to revolve around making our lives easier. We have access to some amazing things in our day. Things happen fast. Results come easier. If we allow it this can creep into our very souls. We want things easy and we want them now.

Patience is hard. There are days when it seems almost impossible. Patience can seem hard for men because there is often an implication that patience involves waiting passively. The inherent suggestion is that a patient man waits kindly without activity or bluster until the proper moment arrives for activity. There may be moments when this is true, but it is the exception not the rule. The world needs men who embrace the difficult task of maintaining patience in the midst of struggle.

Eleazar didn't retreat when his friends did. He held

on. He stood his ground. He fought! This was a man his world needed. There was a place he was unwilling to give up. He refused to back down. He refused to abandon his post, even when it seemed impossible.

Don't aim your life at the impossible out of stubbornness or arrogance. In all things move with wisdom. But don't shy away from what stands between you and your purpose. A man who is capable, full of faith, and knows his purpose is not afraid of the difficulty in front of him. Don't let go! Press on.

Reject the societal pursuit for comfort. Kick complacency in the butt and throw it out of your house. Do the hard things. Make it a habit and you'll have made it your standard. That will begin to change your world.

CHALLENGE: Every time you find yourself becoming impatient today, force yourself to wait thirty more seconds.

6.2 DON'T QUIT

READ: Jeremiah 25:1-38

"For the past twenty-three years—from the thirteenth year of the reign of Josiah son of Amon, king of Judah, until now—the Lord has been giving me his messages. I have faithfully passed them on to you, but you have not listened." Jeremiah 25:3 NLT

There is a misconception in our world that when life is good, life is easy. Deep down we know this is just not true. You weren't designed for an easy life. Sitting by the pool all day or binging your nights away in front of the TV is a waste of your life. You only get one shot at this life. Make the most of it. Embrace your divine design.

You were born for a purpose. You are here for a reason. Your life is not an accident. There is a place and a plan for all of your days. Why? Because the world desperately needs what you bring to the table.

As you step into what you were made for you will begin to encounter incredible difficulties. Most people quit. You can't afford to quit. Because if you put down the thing God has entrusted you with, no one else is going to pick it up. It's your's. God gave it to you. The world needs you to do it.

As men we are all tempted to measure success. When you begin living out your purpose the desire to do this can become strong. Measuring success is not bad, but it can be short-sighted.

You may be handed a situation that is going to require decades of difficulty and strife. Winning may never be defined in a way you are used to. Don't quit. Do keep going. Embrace difficulty. Lean toward it. The man who willingly aims his purpose at the tough stuff is the one who will make a lasting impact.

CHALLENGE: Don't give up today. Even if it seems like you haven't made any traction lately. What is the obstacle in your way? Take another swing at it today.

6.3 LIVE DISCIPLINED

READ: Daniel 1:1-21

For people who hate discipline and only get more stubborn, There'll come a day when life tumbles in and they break, but by then it'll be too late to help them. Proverbs 29:1 MSG

Daniel's world was flipped upside down. He was hauled into a foreign land. His freedom was taken from him. He was made a slave. And still, he persisted. He became the kind of man his world needed.

Faith and trust in God led the way. Daniel overcame much through his dependence on God. But he also demonstrated something remarkable in the face of dire circumstances. Daniel lived with incredible discipline. He managed to live in submission to his masters while remaining true to God and his purpose–at the same time.

You cannot be a man who does hard things without discipline. It cannot be a forced discipline. You must embrace the part of your heart willing to undergo difficulty. Some men achieve an advantage because someone cultivated discipline in them. Perhaps it was your father, a coach, or something you experienced through military service or work. Others find the task of cultivating discipline extremely difficult. Their spirit seems willing, but the flesh is weak.

Living with the discipline to do hard things is a decision only you can make. No one can make it for you. Be willing to be that kind of man. Discipline will cultivate in you a hardness. Not a hardness of heart that will ruin you. Through discipline you will gird your will with an armor that protects you from laziness, temptation, and folly. The disciplined man has the strength to endure what will break weaker men. Which kind do you think your world needs?

CHALLENGE: What is an area of your life that is undisciplined? Is your diet a disaster? Maybe your hobbies are out of control? Examine your life. How can you make one small change today to start moving in the right direction?

6.4 OVERCOME SETBACKS

READ: 1 Kings 19:1-21

> *He said, "I have been very jealous for the Lord, the God of hosts. For the people of Israel have forsaken your covenant, thrown down your altars, and killed your prophets with the sword, and I, even I only, am left, and they seek my life, to take it away." 1 Kings 19:14 ESV*

Elijah experienced an incredible victory over the prophets of Baal quickly followed by an immense setback. The rulers of the land were out for his head. He narrowly escaped with his life. This story reminds us that even those who experienced the supernatural wonders of God had to overcome adversity.

No one gets a free pass. You are going to encounter incredible difficulties. The world is full of people who turn tail and run in the face of difficulty. You were made for overcoming difficulty. From the beginning men have faced moments of extreme hardship.

Difficult moments aren't to be feared. They are certainly not something to ignore. They are something to overcome.

You are capable of more than you may realize. You have what is required to face the hard things you are going to encounter today. You are capable. The world sometimes flinches at the unleashed strength of a fully realized man. The people around you need someone who can show them the way. Someone who will demonstrate what it's like to encounter a setback and press on.

Don't put your head down and try to barrel through hard things. Use wisdom. Know your strengths and abilities. Acknowledge the difficulty while refusing to ignore it. Overcoming the obstacle in front of you will remind you of your ability. The people in your life who need you will rally to your example. Also, it will remind you of your ability when you encounter future setbacks. More difficult things are coming your way. God is with you. You are a man who does hard things.

CHALLENGE: Reflect on a past setback you overcame. How did you grow as a result? Face your current challenges with confidence.

6.5 LET US

READ: Nehemiah 3:1-32

But now I said to them, "You know very well what trouble we are in. Jerusalem lies in ruins, and its gates have been destroyed by fire. Let us rebuild the wall of Jerusalem and end this disgrace!" Nehemiah 2:17 NLT

Too many capable men undermine their own potential by demanding they do everything on their own. Being a man who does hard things will isolate you. Especially in a world full of those who choose the easy path. That doesn't mean you have to do everything on your own.

Do you know what is more difficult than simply picking up a shovel and digging a hole you know you could dig? Gathering some people who may not be ready to dig, and getting them to do it.

The hardest thing you will do is become a man who will challenge those around him to embrace difficulty. But you must. This is not optional. To refuse the mandate to challenge and encourage those around you is to willingly abandon your God-given calling.

To be a man is to lead. To influence. To call up, equip, encourage, resource, and challenge. Your greatest difficulty will be to gather those unwilling to do hard things and teach them how to embrace what they have been unwilling to do.

The world needs you to do this. Your world needs it desperately. You will lead them by example when you live a disciplined life. You will lead them by word when you call them up to it and they follow you. You will lead them by correction when you lovingly instruct how they may have done it better. Your world cannot afford for you to ignore it.

Let us be men willing to gather those God has entrusted to us. Show them the way. Lead the charge. Pick up the tools required for the task ahead. And then do the hardest thing possible—trust someone else to help you do it.

CHALLENGE: Invite someone to help you complete a task you've been avoiding.

DISCUSSION

How do you stay patient in the midst of struggle?

How can you cultivate discipline in an area of your life where you've been struggling?

What is an area in your life where you have been tempted to quit?

How does living with discipline impact those around you, and how can it inspire others?

Have you ever faced a significant setback? How did you respond, and what did you learn from it?

Why is it sometimes more challenging to lead and encourage others to do hard things rather than just doing them yourself?

How can you demonstrate embracing hard things?

How can we create a culture of perseverance and discipline within our group or community?

NOTES

CHAPTER 7
BE A MAN UNAFRAID

"Everything you've ever wanted is on the other side of fear."

~ George Adair

7.1 INTERRUPTED

READ: Psalm 56:1-13

Whenever I am afraid, I will trust in You. Psalm 56:3 NKJV

Everyone is afraid of something. The one insisting they aren't afraid is probably the most afraid. They fear people knowing what they are afraid of. We all fear something, but you don't have to live afraid. Many men wander through their days afraid of failing. No man would volunteer to be the guy who failed to love his wife, raise his kids well, or thrive in his purpose. But millions of men are failing daily. Encouraging isn't it? No! Of course not.

Fear interrupts what God the Father wants for your life. But the truth is—we all struggle with fear. Fear is inevitable. It will show up. But fear does not have to be in control. It is not your boss.

Scripture is full of examples of men who stared into the face of fear. Some of them failed. Others prevailed over their fear. The difference was their reliance on God. David was a man after God's heart, but his failures were rooted in his fears. Moses led the Israelites through incredible circumstances, and his failings also were rooted in his fears.

You are going to be afraid, but it doesn't have to control you. Rather than letting fear determine your steps, trust God. Fear doesn't just melt away because you decide to trust God. Instead, your trust, like your faith, begins to armor you for the inevitable confrontation.

Your world needs a man who is honest about his fears. One who doesn't try to hide them away. Your world needs a man who is not controlled by fear. A man who is an example for those depending on him. Your world needs a man with the kind of strength that only comes through trust.

CHALLENGE: Every time fear shows up today, write the fear on a piece of paper and throw it in the trash.

7.2 GET READY

READ: Jeremiah 1:1-19

Get up and prepare for action. Go out and tell them everything I tell you to say. Do not be afraid of them, or I will make you look foolish in front of them. Jeremiah 1:17 NLT

There is a deviousness that hides behind fear cheering it on. Fear was meant to uproot your ability to do what you were made for. Fear is a learned behavior. So is fearlessness.

When you are afraid you have an opportunity. It becomes a valuable moment. It's a chance to climb above the fetid terror longing to grip your heart. When fear reaches for you, you can throw off its grasp.

You are capable. You trust God. You have faith. You were made for this. God put everything inside of you that you will need to counter the terrible fears in your life. They are already there. As you trust God and walk each day with Him they will begin to be refined and revealed. The habits and tools you require to overcome the crazy power of fear are not only within reach, they are inside you. The heart of a man is an invention that predates the existence of fear. Your timeless masculinity is a powerful force God made that existed long before fear began to grab up mankind.

Fear is going to show up. Probably today. Or, maybe it never really left. If you allow it to grip you, it will interrupt everything you are supposed to do. It will thwart, delay, or derail all God intends for you to accomplish in your world.

Your world needs you to get up and get ready. Don't wait. You don't need permission. There is a fierce power inside your beating heart. One God made. Fear has nothing on that. Fear is not your master. God's purpose is before you. The world needs you. All you have to do is get up and get ready.

CHALLENGE: Take five minutes to prepare yourself for the fears you are going to face today. How did you overcome them in the past?

7.3 POWERLESS

READ: 2 Timothy 1:1-18

"For the Spirit God gave us does not make us timid, but gives us power, love and self-discipline."
2 Timothy 1:7 NIV

The powerless man is one gripped by his fear. It controls him. He backs down at every turn. This isn't humility. It is passivity and cowardice.

Timidity and humility are not the same. However, we live in a world that confuses the two daily. The world would push timidity on you and call it humility. Nonsense. The humble man knows his strength and walks in it. He lives with the power of purpose God fashioned in his heart. And, he gives credit and deference to the one who gave it to him.

The Spirit of God inside you defies timidity. God will not be afraid. You should not either.

There is incredible power available to the man who is no longer afraid. This becomes apparent over time. Discipline is the fruit of an unafraid life. The man who is no longer afraid is willing to carve out the dedication it takes to become a man the world needs.

Because fear can't hold you down you will rise. You will rise to accomplish all that God puts before you.

You will do it with His help. You will do it with real humility. A humility born of the powerful strength God put inside you. You will accomplish it because you love your world. You love your family, friends, and neighbors. You know they need what God has given you. Fear won't stop you because you are dedicated to living the disciplined life it requires to bring your God-given purpose to a world in need.

CHALLENGE: Identify an area where you have been passive. Today, go right at it with bold decisive action.

7.4 JUST SEE

READ: 2 Kings 6:1-33

> *"Don't be afraid!" Elisha told him. "For there are more on our side than on theirs!"* 2 Kings 6:16 NLT

Our world runs on fear. The economy is driven by fear. People are afraid so they buy things in an attempt to preempt fear. Politics is a diseased cesspool of fear. All too often it seems to degenerate into groups of opinionated blowhards selling their preferred brand of fear. The industrial military complex, the pharmaceutical industry, even software and online safeguards—much of it runs on fear.

The fears you bow to will run your life. If you let fear into your home it will become a permanent resident. Don't let it in. People in your world are depending on you to stop it cold.

When we don't, here is what happens. The fears pile up. Rational fears, like being mindful of heights, or the consequences of eating a terrible diet, become displaced by irrational fears like how your latest social media post is performing and whether or not someone likes your haircut.

If you do not accept your own responsibility for

your fears, you will always be afraid. You will be a victim of your fears—no matter their rationale. They will become the invisible masters circling your every decision and moment. It will become suffocating.

Here is a truth far too many people won't accept. There is nothing to fear and every reason to be careful. Carefulness is what happens when you move through your days with wisdom. Embrace carefulness. Reject fear.

What if you didn't have to be afraid anymore? You don't. And your world needs you to live unafraid. Pray for your eyes to be opened to this reality. You are capable, and you are not alone.

CHALLENGE: Pray this prayer: "God, help me today to see all the reasons I have to live unafraid."

7.5 THE OTHER SIDE

READ: Mark 4:1-41

On that day, when evening had come, he said to them, "Let us go across to the other side." Mark 4:35 ESV

Fear will stop you in your tracks. If you let it. That's the dangerous thing about fear. It has the power to turn men passive, but only if we give it permission.

What if the disciples had decided not to go with Jesus? It seems almost unthinkable to consider, right? These are the disciples we're talking about! Christianity as we know it wouldn't exist without them. But guess what? They got in the boat when Jesus said, "let's go." Sometimes God is saying, "C'mon let's go." And we're too afraid to take the next step. Your world needs a man who is unafraid.

God is not sending you into a future full of small things. His plan for you is too important. His love for you is too big. There are going to be some storms in front of you. Because that's where the biggest possibilities live. There are some strongholds to conquer because that's where freedom finds the greatest potential.

It can be difficult to admit our fears. And, it seems

like men struggle with this more. Men struggle with fear because they are trying to get it right. If you struggle with fear it's likely because you want to be a good dad, husband, employee, leader—fill in the blank.

The disciples had no idea of the storm they were sailing into. But they did know that Jesus had said, "follow me." You are going to have trouble. You are going to face problems. You are going to run into head-winds that will seem to stall your plans, stir up your fear, and tempt you to quit. It's in those moments when you must remember what Jesus says to all who choose to follow him with their lives, "let us go across to the other side."

On the other side of your fear is where your world needs you. It may seem impossible to get there. It is not. Just by making the attempt you will begin to make a difference in the lives of those who need you.

CHALLENGE: Go to the other side of your fear today. Whatever you have been afraid of, it is time to face it.

DISCUSSION

What fears do you encounter the most? How can acknowledging your fears help you overcome them?

How does fear influence the decisions you make in your daily life? How can preparation help you?

How do you differentiate between timidity and humility?

How can embracing carefulness instead of fear lead to a less anxiety-driven life?

Reflect on a time when fear stopped you from taking a significant step. How did it feel, and what was the outcome?

Share a personal story where you confronted a significant fear. What was the outcome, and what did you learn from the experience?

Who are some role models of fearlessness in your life? What characteristics did they exhibit that you admire?

NOTES

CHAPTER 8
BE A MAN WHO IS DIFFERENT

"When the whole world is running towards a cliff, he who is running in the opposite direction appears to have lost his mind."

~ C.S. Lewis

8.1 DON'T CONFORM

READ: Romans 12:1-21

Do not conform to the pattern of this world, but be transformed by the renewing of your mind. Then you will be able to test and approve what God's will is—his good, pleasing and perfect will. Romans 12:2 NIV

"Just go with the flow" is some of the worst advice you can receive. Don't do it. The laissez faire approach to life is reckless, stupid, and disastrous. It will undermine your heart and what God wants for you.

You were built to be different. This starts with our heart. We have to desire to be different. If our thoughts are constantly focused on attaining the same things the people around us strive for, we will find ourselves caught in the same trappings of life. And it is a trap. Believe that. Stand apart. Stand out. Rise above it. You were always meant to.

Your desire to be different from the world around you will reinforce your identity as a son of God. This desire inside you will stoke your willpower. Your refusal to conform will strengthen.

Take a good look around you. If your life is just like everyone else's you're missing the mark. You were always meant to be different. Unfortunately, this is easier said than done. We need daily reminders. Everyday we have to resolve to live set apart all over again. Everyday we must refocus our aim. Remind yourself every morning of what really matters.

Your life is an opportunity to set the standard. Be the example. Getting this right gives you agency. You have a free will. You're not a robot. God's gift inside of you comes with the ability and the opportunity to figure things out for yourself. Check your desires against those that line up with what God wants for the world around you. Where the two meet you are likely to discover precisely what God wishes for you as His son. Your world is desperately in need of a man willing to figure out how his desires will help those around him.

CHALLENGE: Evaluate your life. How are you the same as the other men around you? Is this a good thing? Or, are you caught up in the same meaningless stuff? Are you conforming to the pattern of this world? Be honest.

8.2 GIVE YOURSELF

READ: 1 Corinthians 15:1-58

Therefore, my dear brothers and sisters, stand firm. Let nothing move you. Always give yourselves fully to the work of the Lord, because you know that your labor in the Lord is not in vain. 1 Corinthians 15:58 NIV

Have you noticed this disturbing trend during bowl season in recent years? Football players are repeatedly opting out of playing with their team in the big game. We hear a lot of excuses about it. Mostly they boil down to players not wanting to hinder their prospects for whatever might be next. This is such a tragedy. These young men train all their lives to be excellent, and when their time to shine arrives they pull back.

When we put ourselves first it becomes all too easy to disengage if the payoff doesn't seem to center around our own wishes. You were built to be different. Don't worry about taking center stage. Concern yourself with serving your world. Make it better. You will begin to shine where you are. Give yourself to it fully.

There are a lot of lazy selfish people in this world. Don't be one of them. Work. Work hard. If something is worth doing, it is worth doing well. Give yourself to it. Go hard. All the way to the finish line. Give it all you've got.

Pride, vanity, and greed go hand in hand. They are the beginnings of all that went wrong in our world. They run rampant through the lives of so many. Pride, vanity, and greed are so common in our time they have become acceptable. This has led to a type of cultural narcissism. What a shame.

You are a man who is different. Aim yourself at a worthy goal. The work before you is the work God has entrusted to you. Go for it. Give yourself to it.

CHALLENGE: Today take on a task that you don't have to do. Do it just to serve and help someone. Look for no reward or gratitude, only the sense of having done the work well.

8.3 NO EXCUSES

READ: Exodus 32:1-35

So I said to them, 'Let any who have gold take it off.' So they gave it to me, and I threw it into the fire, and out came this calf." Exodus 32:24 ESV

Moses had gone up onto the mountain. While he was gone the people of Israel grew restless. They gave into their impulses and wicked nature. Rather than standing up for what was right, Aaron gave in to their whims. He made an idol for them to worship. Aaron failed his people. He failed them when he gave into their wickedness. Aaron failed them when he didn't take responsibility for his actions. He failed his people when he made excuses for what he had done. He blamed the people he had been entrusted to lead rather than accepting responsibility for what he had done wrong.

The world needs men who refuse to make excuses. You are responsible for your actions—no one else. You are responsible for what you decide to do. You are responsible for what you are complicit in. You are responsible for your own complacency. Either by action or inaction, you bear responsibility for the consequences of the wicked things you allow in your life.

Be a man who is different. Don't give in to excuses. Don't give into the fickle bemoaning of the confused mob. The mob will always default to evil. A man who has not resolved to be different will be swept away in it.

A man who is different will stand like a mighty oak when faced by the flood of cultural wickedness. Even when others demand acceptance for what is wrong, you *must* stand up for what is right. Fair warning. When you take a righteous stand it reminds the wicked how evil they are. They will hate you for it. They hated Jesus.

We all sin. Don't make excuses. That's just another false god. It's another way of worshiping your own selfishness. You are a man who is different. You are the example your world needs. When you make a mistake, you don't hide it, accept responsibility. In this world people refuse to accept truth and responsibility until it is too late. You will be different.

CHALLENGE: What is the most recent thing that went wrong in your life? Write down three reasons why you think it happened. Evaluate the list. Are you taking ownership, or are you making excuses?

8.4 THE RIGHT TROUBLE

READ: 1 Kings 18:1-46

> *The moment Ahab saw Elijah he said, "So it's you, old troublemaker!" 1 Kings 18:17 MSG*

The man who is different is not willing to go along with the disastrous decisions of the day. The prophet Elijah had a reputation for this. He was a troublemaker.

It's unlikely you and I will be tasked with the same kind of dissent Elijah was characterized for. But, you never know. The details are less important than the intent. Elijah obeyed God out of intent and out of his nature. He was a man willing to be different. He was a man unwilling to go along with the evil of the day.

You and I are living in a time when some good things are labeled as evil by the wicked forces of culture. In the same breath vile practices are promoted as acceptable and, even preferred, behaviors.

Radical sexual, marriage, and gender norms, identity politics, subversion of authentic human rights, abortion, and so many other issues of our day have been conflated and corrupted. The world needs men who refuse to bow to the Baals of our day. Men willing to stand up in a crowd and call down fire should the occasion demand it. If you felt the weight of that, good! Being a man the world needs is a heavy responsibility. One we should never take lightly. One we should continually seek the Lord's help to fulfill.

Jesus was peaceful, mostly, but he wasn't passive. They didn't murder him for being passive. The elites murdered Jesus because he was a troublemaker. The man who makes trouble just for the sake of stirring the pot misses the point entirely. That's not a man the world needs. That's a man seeking attention. We don't need more narcissists. Your world needs men willing to stand against the tide of wicked chaos overrunning our world. Your world needs a man who is different. One willing to make the right trouble.

CHALLENGE: There is nothing to be gained by keeping your mouth shut when everyone around you decides to go with the flow. If the opportunity to stand for what's right causes you to stand out today, embrace it.

8.5 BE GREAT

READ: Matthew 20:1-34

> *"Not so with you. Instead, whoever wants to become great among you must be your servant, and whoever wants to be first must be your slave— just as the Son of Man did not come to be served, but to serve, and to give his life as a ransom for many." Matthew 20:26-28 NIV*

When my Aunt JoAnn passed away people lined up outside the funeral home in my small hometown for hours to pay their respects. Hundreds of people passed through. I had never seen anything like this before despite having cared for many families during times of loss. Why did they come? They came to pay respects to someone who was great. Someone who was known as a bright light in her community. Someone who served others endlessly.

One of the greatest gifts we can receive as men is when we recognize this beautiful truth about life. Life is not about us. Living selfishly robs people of the incredible life they could be living. How do we avoid this? Choose to better the world around you instead of chasing vain egotism.

Jesus made it clear. Greatness lies in service, not

selfishness. The one willing to forgo self will rise above the clamoring noise of selfishness.

Selfishness causes our thoughts to betray us. We become focused, totally consumed, on pursuing avenues for attaining our desires. Serving others is a different way to live. It is a better way to live.

Be a man willing to be different. Aim your efforts at aiding those around you. Make their lives better. Improve this world. Leverage your incredible capacity in a direction that will impact the world for good. Reject the path that serves only you. Identify a direction that helps the people in front of you. Go for it. You will be great.

CHALLENGE: Look for the selfless choice today. When it shows up, embrace it. If you do it everyday it will become a habit.

DISCUSSION

Share an example of a time when you chose to stand out rather than conform. What was the outcome?

What did you learn from a recent mistake? When are you most tempted to make excuses? Why?

How do you determine when it is necessary to take a stand against cultural norms?

What does it mean to you to be a servant leader?

Who do you admire for their selflessness? How can you emulate them?

How do you handle criticism or backlash when you choose to stand out and be different from those around you?

How do you balance standing firm in your convictions with showing compassion and understanding to others who may disagree with you?

What kind of legacy do you want to leave behind as a man who chose to be different? How are you working towards that legacy today?

NOTES

CHAPTER 9
BE A MAN WHO IMPROVES

"There is nothing noble in being superior to your fellow man; true nobility is being superior to your former self."

~ Ernest Hemingway

9.1 POTENTIAL

READ: Judges 6:1-40

And the angel of the Lord appeared to him and said to him, "The Lord is with you, O mighty man of valor." Judges 6:12 ESV

There is something incredible about being believed in. When someone believes in your ability, or even your potential, it shifts something inside of you. I hope you have experienced this at least once in your life. The difference between who you are and who you could be is the measure of your potential.

God's view of you is not limited by time. That is amazing! God saw the valorous warrior in Gideon before he ever saw it in himself. Indeed, before he had become a warrior at all.

God's not surprised by what's inside of you. He planted the seeds of your potential. It will take time and intentionality in order to see it grow. You can do it. Your world needs you to.

There will be many obstacles on the path before you. As a man who does hard things you're not intimidated by them. Choose to see them for what they are. They aren't impediments to the life God wants for you, they are opportunities to demonstrate what you're made of.

We all battle some level of imposter syndrome. Don't do what Gideon did. Don't place conditions on your potential. Don't play around with doubting your own capabilities. You are capable. You are a man the world needs. You were made for it.

Begin by believing. There's nothing wrong with believing in yourself. Taking pride in your capability is only dangerous when you try to pretend you did it all on your own. Your potential is the fertile soil of improvement. It's where God wants you to go. It is how much God wants you to grow. Your potential points the way forward with Him. Aim high and aim your life at what your world needs.

CHALLENGE: Ask someone close to you to describe an area of your life where you have untapped potential.

9.2 THE RIGHT INCREASE

READ: Luke 2:1-52

And Jesus increased in wisdom and in stature and in favor with God and man. Luke 2:52 ESV

Jesus was the ultimate man. In every sense he came to be the man the world needed. As the son of God he always was this man. As a young Hebrew boy he had to increase in a way that led to the divine moments he was born for.

Jesus' apparent increase doesn't discount his innate ability and identity. He was the son of God. He was born to be the savior of the world. He was also the son of a poor craftsman in a small town in an impoverished village.

Every man I know wants his lot in life to increase. We all want things to improve for the people we care about. When we get this desire right we want it more for the people in our world than for ourselves. This certainly seemed to be the case with Jesus. Everything he said and did was focused on serving those in need, even to his death—which served everyone.

As with so many aspects of our life as men, we need to aim for the right increase. Desire to improve. You have innate God-given abilities. Long to grow in those things. Get better at the stuff you're already good at. Be intentional in your pursuit of improvement.

It's easy to tell what a man cares about. He spends time with it. The one who values golf works on his golf swing. The hunter strives to be a better marksman. Identify what matters to you. Determine what you want to see increase concerning your character, your ability, and your opportunities. Once you know, invest time in them.

People don't improve by accident. It's in our nature to coast. Coasting will cost you everything when it comes to advancement. You won't get better by accident. You will get worse. If you choose not to improve, you have actually chosen to falter.

The world is always changing. There will always be a need for your abilities. Your skill is a gift from God to your world. Don't be complacent, be intentional. Aim for the right kind of increase in your life, and unleash your gifts on a world in need.

CHALLENGE: Spend 15 minutes every day this week developing the potential revealed in the last challenge.

9.3 GROW

READ: 1 Timothy 4:1-16

"For physical training is of some value, but godliness has value for all things, holding promise for both the present life and the life to come." 1 Timothy 4:8 NIV

One day at center court Coach Parrish called us together and taught us one of his simple maxims that I have never forgotten, "Men, you're either going to climb the ladder or fall, you can't just hang on." What did he mean? We were meant to be men who improve.

When you study the way our bodies work it reveals this truth. Every fiber of your physical being is designed with the potential to excel. Your bodies are incredible machines capable of wonders. But growth doesn't happen by accident. You won't stumble into improvement.

The world is full of weak passive men. Some of them have decided to take the "easy" path. So they do nothing. Their days are cycles of mindless pleasure consumed by video games and other trite frivolities. Some men genuinely don't know any better because no one ever showed them the way. You are neither kind of man.

You are a man who has embraced God's design for you. As everyone else yearns to make life easier, you are embracing the reality of life's hardship. There are no easy streets. Easy street has always been a lie vomited straight out of the pit of hell.

You were designed to be capable. Your ability was hardwired into your very nature. Reject the complacency of our day. Strive headlong against the tide. Grow into the man who will accomplish the task set before you.

Grow in strength. Train your body to become stronger, to the best of your ability. Train your mind to become shrewd. Allow wisdom to guide your decisions. Train your heart to love the people around you. Train your soul to lean toward hope. You will grow in these things as you do them.

As you grow in strength, ability, love, and wisdom don't neglect to grow in godliness. Pursue what God wants for your world. Embrace potential. It is precisely what your world needs.

CHALLENGE: Pray this prayer, "God, help me grow closer to you this week. Show me an area of my life where I can be stronger through your help."

9.4 REJECT INSECURITY

READ: 1 Samuel 16:1-23

*So Samuel took the horn of oil and anointed him in
the presence of his brothers, and from that day on
the Spirit of the Lord came powerfully upon David.*
1 Samuel 16:13 NIV

Israel's first king was a disappointment. King Saul
did not lead the people toward God. He led them out
of his own insecurity. Insecurity always short circuits
the opportunity to make a lasting impact on your
world. Insecurity makes a man see everything through
the lens of his own importance. This is a recipe for
disaster.

God saw the potential in David. But, there was a
season between David's anointing and taking the
throne. Some things needed to happen in David for
him to be the king his world needed. David grew and
changed. When we first read about David he is a
capable young man. He became an incredible man. He
became a man the world needed.

Still, David was a flawed man. We are all flawed
men. It's easy to gloss over his failures. It's also easy to
point fingers. David was a man his world needed. He
excelled in many of the areas where the need was

great. He also failed miserably in some of life's most essential areas. He seems to have been a terrible father and husband. But he was known as an incredible warrior and king.

When you examine David's failures they usually revolve around the same core problems Saul had. David dealt with some insecurity. When David was at his best he is remembered as "A man after God's own heart." He was the guy who often pursued what God himself desired.

Reject the insecurity of our day. Don't make it all about you. Don't make it about your wins or your losses. Don't focus on your inadequacies or your inherent qualities. Instead, focus on becoming the man your world needs you to be. Be the king you need to be where you're called to lead. Be the warrior your world needs when there is a worthy fight in front of you. Be the father and husband your family desperately needs. Don't pick and choose. Your world needs you. If that sounds impossible, that's because it is. You can't do it alone. You will need God to help you be the man your world needs.

CHALLENGE: What have you been avoiding? That's the face of your insecurity. You have to move to eliminate your insecurity. Today, take a step toward facing the thing in your life you have been avoiding.

9.5 HOLY GROUND

READ: Exodus 3:1-22

> *"The Israelite cry for help has come to me, and I've seen for myself how cruelly they're being treated by the Egyptians. It's time for you to go back: I'm sending you to Pharaoh to bring my people, the People of Israel, out of Egypt." Exodus 3: 9-10 MSG*

Moses fled Egypt at forty years old. He got married, had kids, and built a life. Four decades passed and when Moses was tending sheep he saw a burning bush.

Moses wound up on that mountain because God had a plan for him. It took Moses forty years in exile to become the man God was going to send back to Egypt. Moses kept tending his sheep, and caring for his family. Moses kept taking small steps of faithfulness. One day God said, "I want you to take a big step."

Trust and leadership take time to develop. In a world full of video calls and DoorDash anything that doesn't happen immediately seems archaic. The impact on our hearts has been an almost wholesale abandonment of delayed gratification.

Everything worth doing takes time. Growth takes

time. Improvement takes time. Being a man of faith and capacity means trusting God over the long haul. Reject the desire to pursue short sighted instant "success".   Remember, Moses left the palace for the brickyard.

When you choose what is good over what is immediate you will look insane. However, what looks like exile to the world around you may actually be your proving grounds. What your world sees as monotony is actually the opportunity of a lifetime. Strength and trust are never instantaneous. They are muscles. They require the slow and steady improvement that only comes through daily faithfulness.

Your family, your job, your routines, and the apparent minutiae of your life aren't in your way, they are the way. Your world doesn't need another man caught up in the fickle fashionable pursuit of instant success. Your world needs a man committed to an advancement measured in decades. The path to the holy ground is the proving ground.

CHALLENGE: What has seemed frustrating and difficult lately? Pray this prayer, "God, help me to see the opportunity in my struggle. As I navigate the hardship, help me grow into the man my world needs."

DISCUSSION

In what areas of your life do you feel you have the most potential for growth?

Have you ever experienced someone believing in your potential? How did it impact you?

What does it mean to you to aim for the right kind of increase in your life? How do you deal with imposter syndrome?

How do you identify what truly matters to you and ensure you are investing time in those areas?

What habits or routines have you found most effective in avoiding complacency and fostering improvement?

In what ways do you strive to grow in strength, ability, love, and wisdom?

What steps can you take today to move toward eliminating an insecurity or challenge you have been avoiding?

NOTES

_____

_____

_____

_____

_____

_____

_____

_____

_____

_____

_____

_____

_____

_____

_____

_____

_____

_____

_____

_____

_____

_____

CHAPTER 10
BE A MAN WHO EMPOWERS

"I will prepare and someday my chance will come"

~ Abraham Lincoln

10.1 IN PLAIN SIGHT

READ: Deuteronomy 31:1-30

> *Then Moses summoned Joshua and said to him in the sight of all Israel, "Be strong and courageous, for you shall go with this people into the land that the Lord has sworn to their fathers to give them, and you shall put them in possession of it. Deuteronomy 31:7 ESV*

Moses had led the Israelites for forty years. They had been through some incredible stuff together. God had done miraculous things. And, the time had come for what was next. Only, Moses wasn't the man for the job. As amazing as his leadership had been, it took a different leader for the next part of God's plan.

Few things are as rewarding in leadership as passing the torch. Being given the opportunity to empower the one who comes after you is such a blessing. As a trusted leader you have a unique opportunity to shift public trust toward your replacement. When this is handled well it sets up the next guy for success. When it is botched it becomes some kind of secretive affair.

Maybe you are in your prime. You are leading your family, organization, or business—and doing an incredible job. Don't ignore the succession. If you love what you have built, prepare the next generation. Don't do it in a corner out of sight. Do it with care and intentionality. Do it in the open.

Leaders who hold on for too long are leaders who lose. They lose the incredible gift of investing in the next leader. They lose the satisfaction of praying and dreaming over possibilities that lay beyond their reach. They lose the gift of giving trust, authority, and opportunity to the next guy the world needs.

CHALLENGE: Identify one person in your life you can begin preparing for a larger responsibility.

10.2 THE HAND OFF

READ: Numbers 27:1-23

So the Lord said to Moses, "Take Joshua the son of Nun, a man in whom is the Spirit, and lay your hand on him." Numbers 27:18 ESV

Moses had taken the people as far he could. He had reached the end of his journey. But he lived to see the end of the road. The Promise Land lay before the people. Moses knew that he was not the one to lead his people into their next season. That honor was to be Joshua's. Imagine how Moses must have felt to see the man he had long relied on coming into such an important role in the lives of their people.

Succession is an important conversation in any leadership journey. Too many leaders don't begin to think about it until it's too late. But a great marker of any great leader is their willingness to empower future leaders.

It takes so many different aspects working together in the heart of a man to help him empower others. Insecurity has to be nonexistent. A strong desire to see the world improve has to be the norm. Trust, faith, hope, and consideration are all part of the process.

Having the opportunity to invest in the next leader is an incredible gift. Being able to set them up for success is rewarding. Be a man who strives for both. Be a man who empowers others.

You are a man the world needs. And, you are capable of training men the world needs. You have the right stuff. But, you don't have to do it all alone. In fact, if you try to do everything you are actually hindering more than helping. At some point a man has to acknowledge that the world needs him to hand it off to the next generation.

If you believe in the difference you've been called to make in this world, look for someone willing to give it a shot. Give them a chance. Show them the ropes. Coach them. Help them. Every Moses has Joshua waiting. Just as you were called at the burning bush, he has been commissioned by the Holy Spirit. The world needs men ready to empower the next one.

CHALLENGE: Today, call or meet with the one you are mentoring. Discuss one thing you can do to prepare them to take ownership of something that has been your responsibility in the past.

10.3 CREATE OPPORTUNITY

READ: 2 Kings 2:1-25

And so it was, when they had crossed over, that Elijah said to Elisha, "Ask! What may I do for you, before I am taken away from you?" 2 Kings 2:9 NKJV

Leadership requires trust. When you decide to follow someone it is an act of trust. When a leader empowers someone it is also an act of trust. Both parties are demonstrating mutual trust.

Elijah trusted Elisha to follow him. Elisha trusted in Elijah's leadership. Both men demonstrated a powerful leadership example that holds up hundreds of years later. Taking your place within the ranks of leadership is not about advancement. It is not about getting what you deserve. Becoming a leader is about becoming someone capable of being trusted.

As a trusted leader it is imperative we demonstrate trust in others. An important way we demonstrate this is when we empower others. The weakest man is the one who has no one to rely on. It is a weak man who assumes he must do it all himself. The man who tries to do it all has been deceived. He believes he can do it all alone. He assumes he must do it all. A man who tries to do it all alone often assumes he is the best one for the job. The world doesn't need any more men living out these assumptions.

Be a man who is intentional about giving someone a shot. Let them learn. Let them try. How else can they ever improve?

Insecurity and selfishness are toxic traits that exist on some level in almost every man. We all must face them. Deal with insecurity and selfishness quickly. Address them in yourself first. Do it with zero tolerance. One of the best ways to undermine your own insecurity is to create opportunities for others to lead. Be a man who trusts those around him with leadership. You may be more skilled in an area, but don't leverage your skill in order to horde opportunities. Use your ability to create learning opportunities for those who trust you.

CHALLENGE: Today is the day. Trust the one you mentor. It's time for him to get a shot. He should do it with you on hand to encourage and coach. Help him improve for the next time.

10.4 GIVE COURAGE

READ: Hebrews 3:1-19

But encourage one another daily, as long as it is called "Today," so that none of you may be hardened by sin's deceitfulness. Hebrews 3:13 NIV

Sin is tricky because there is a masterful force behind it. Deception is something no man can afford to live with. But the root of deception goes all the way back to the beginning. Eve was deceived. Adam stood right there watching. Where was his courage?

We all need brotherhood. We need other men who are willing to call out weakness in us. Not because we are looking for opportunities to ridicule one another. Shame is toxic. We were meant to be men who encourage each other.

You won't always have the courage you need. But your brother may. He won't always have the courage he needs. You can take up the slack. Resolve to be a man willing to give courage.

The mutual courage of a brotherhood becomes like an armor for your soul. A destructive life will harden your heart to life's goodness. But the armor of courage will protect your heart. The man who knows the brotherhood of courage is valiant enough to stay tender to the goodness of life's sweetest moments.

We hear the term "toxic masculinity" a lot in our day. It's an overused oversimplification. If anything, toxic masculinity is the byproduct of a man whose heart has become calloused to life's sweet moments. You were never designed to become so macho you brush off the beauty of this world. That's not masculinity. And it's not courage. It's a recipe for disaster.

Be a man who lifts others up with his words. Let your talk be seasoned with syllables that prop up the people around you. Your banter should embolden them. Courage isn't a pep talk. It's what happens when one man the world needs tells another man he is what the world needs, and they both know it to be true.

CHALLENGE: Share your courage with someone today. Encourage them.

10.5 SATISFIED

READ: Exodus 18:1-27

"If you do this and God so commands, you will be able to stand the strain, and all these people will go home satisfied." Exodus 18:23 NIV

Moses faced many crises in his leadership of the Israelites. They faced physical hardships. They were establishing a new society. Moses was helping the people learn their spiritual identity. And of course, they were experiencing the complexities of navigating the wilderness with a large population. Throw into the mix normal relational squabbles and it was a recipe for leadership overload.

Moses' father in law Jethro gave great advice. Leadership is not a one man show. It's not a solo sport. Leadership is meant to be shared.

Moses empowered men in his company to lead the people. He showed incredible wisdom. He used his God-given authority to give others the ability to lead. Trust was distributed. But Moses didn't just push leadership off on someone else and leave them to it. Moses sought God's help, and he listened. The Law that would guid the people for centuries to come was the result.

Be a man who trusts and empowers others to lead. If you're truly doing what God has set before you to do, it is too big for you to do alone. Trust others to help you carry the load. But don't just shove it off on them. Teach them. You will have experienced the joy that comes through empowering another to live their calling. The end result will be better for everyone.

Many hands make light work. You will do more when you trust more. You will do less when you trust less. Be a man who empowers others.

CHALLENGE: Today when the opportunity comes to do a leadership task yourself, look for someone else you can trust to do it. Share the load. Empower them. Look for an opportunity to talk about it after.

DISCUSSION

How do you prepare yourself for future opportunities? How do you encourage others to do the same?

Have you ever been in a position to pass the torch to someone else? How did it feel?

What steps do you take to create opportunities for others to lead and grow?

How do you address and overcome insecurity in your own leadership journey?

What does mutual trust look like in your leadership style? How do you build it with others?

How do you balance the need to lead with the need to empower others to take on leadership roles?

How do you encourage and support your peers or subordinates in their personal and professional growth?

What strategies do you use to share the load of leadership and avoid burnout?

NOTES

_____

_____

_____

_____

_____

_____

_____

_____

_____

_____

_____

_____

_____

_____

_____

_____

_____

_____

_____

_____

_____

CHAPTER 11
BE A MAN WHO IS FREE

"Where the battle rages, there the loyalty of the soldier is proved."

~ Martin Luther

11.1 WEAK SPOTS

READ: Matthew 26:1-75

> *Watch and pray that you may not enter into temptation. The spirit indeed is willing, but the flesh is weak. Matthew 26:41 ESV*

As much as we would love to believe we are invincible, we must be honest. We are all flawed men. Perfection is beyond our means. Failure is inevitable. As long as we are breathing there is a chance for failure. We have a weakness. We all have it. The curse Adam brought down upon humanity is as ingrained in us as our potential for goodness.

Even so, you don't have to give in to your impulses. They don't get to boss you around, unless you allow them to. A man must learn to fight his weakness. Sometimes this involves willpower. We can hone this with discipline and practice. Sometimes we fight our weaknesses through our habits and routines. Build your desired life around your strengths. Attempt to leave out room for your weaknesses. We can also fight our weaknesses by banding together. Join a brotherhood of men capable of calling out the best in you.

The worst thing we can do is to pretend our weakness is nonexistent. The world needs honest men. That includes being willing to be honest about weakness. Having a trusted friend or group you can be open with about your weakness is a lifeline.

On the journey to being a man the world needs we want to strive for honesty. Take a good long honest look at the man in the mirror. Perhaps it is even time to get a friend in on the conversation. Be a man willing to be honest about his weakness.

CHALLENGE: What do you think your biggest weakness is? Is it obvious? Is it secretive? Consider asking a close friend for their input.

11.2 NO OPPORTUNITY

READ: Luke 4:1-44

And when the devil had ended every temptation, he departed from him until an opportune time.
Luke 4:13 ESV

One of my favorite stories is the story of Jesus being tempted. Because the curtain is pulled back a bit more to show Jesus' humanity. He was tired. He was hungry. He was human. And, just like you and I, he was tempted.

Jesus thwarted temptation. He stopped the devil in his tracks, repeatedly. Satan took shots at Jesus fatigue from his time fasting in the wilderness. Satan tried to pry a gap in Christ's ego and identity. He couldn't find a foothold. The Son of God was prepared.

You are a son of God. Temptation is not your master. You don't have to give in to it. And, you can bet that it is going to show up today. Nothing will undercut your big purpose in this world faster than guilt and shame. Temptation is the crack that gives evil its opportunity. Deny it even a finger hold.

Jesus rejected the advances of the enemy and Luke wrote that the devil left until "an opportune time". Forever after Satan was trying to figure out a way to tempt Jesus. The agony of Christ's final temptation was manifested in the garden. Jesus wrestled with his own human desire to avoid the suffering he knew was coming. Jesus won.

You are a son of God. You can bet that your enemy is right there. He's waiting for the opportune time. Your enemy will try his best to deceive you right out of the good plan God has for you.

The man who is free is the one where temptation finds no opportunity. The man who is free is the one where selfishness has no chance. The man who is free is the one willing to lay down his life for those around him. The most extreme form of selflessness possible is the ultimate armor against the opportunity evil craves. When you are willing to lay it all down in the service of those you love—you are truly free.

CHALLENGE: Evaluate your habits in light of your weaknesses. You know what they are. Identify a habit you have that is creating the opportunity for temptation to strike.

11.3 YOU WILL

READ: John 8:1-59

"And ye shall know the truth, and the truth shall make you free." John 8:32 NIV

In November 1961 Allen Dulles, director of the Central Intelligence Agency insisted Jesus' words be inscribed upon the stone wall of the C.I.A. 's new headquarters. Six decades later, Jesus' words about freedom being the unofficial motto of the keeper of national secrets seems more than ironic. Irony aside, the words of Jesus as recorded by John the Beloved are packed with promise.

The promise that waits in this simple statement is profound. You and I can know the truth. Truth is something we can experience. It is something we can attain intellectually. Truth also goes beyond experience. Truth resonates with us. As men of God, truth is someone we can know. Jesus is the truth that makes us free.

One of the saddest moments in human history was the moment Pontious Pilate stood face to face with Jesus and asked "what is truth?" There he stood in the presence of the Truth who had come to free him, and yet he did not recognize it.

Today you and I live in a time of great delusions. Radical ideologies abound. Especially around the topics of sexuality and gender. People have become slaves to their delusions. The pursuit of reckless selfishness has chained them to a wanton disregard for truth. The rise of "my truth" is evidence of this.

Truth is not fluid. Truth is reality. What Jesus wanted his friends to know is the same thing he is hoping you and I will come to understand. If we know him, we will be made free.

Living life anchored in Christ frees us from the deception of selfishness. When Christ is made king of your life there will be no more room for being subjugated to selfishness. Everyone serves a king. Either we serve King Jesus and the truth is made open to us, or we serve our own delusions. Which kind of man does the world need?

CHALLENGE: Is there a lie you used to believe about yourself? What was it? Are there any echoes of the lie you still need freedom from? Take a moment to pray and meditate on this.

11.4 FOR FREEDOM

READ: Galatians 5:1-26

Christ has set us free to live a free life. So take your stand! Never again let anyone put a harness of slavery on you. Galatians 5:1 MSG

Human history is stained by the tragedy of slavery. It is a dark blight on the reputation of mankind. Certainly our nation is not innocent of this horrific truth. It is hard to fathom a greater form of wickedness than the one that convinces a man he might own another person like they were property.

You were born to live a free life. You were designed with God-given agency. You have freewill. Live in your freedom.

There are many things in your life that would jump at the chance to chain you. It doesn't take long to look around and see a tide of men chained to their work, hobbies, insecurities, and vices. Listen, your past is not your future.

The chances of someone putting literal chains of slavery on you are pretty slim. But that doesn't exclude men from enslaving themselves daily. They are slaves to pornography, alcohol, work, and narcissism. As men we have the capacity for incredible selfishness.

Looking back, Adam's choice to sin was a selfish choice. He would rather have stayed united with the beautiful woman Eve, than obey God. Many of us have made similar choices.

When we choose what we want over what God desires we are chaining ourselves. We are becoming slaves to our fallen nature. Jesus has set you free. He did it so you would live free.

The world needs men who will stand for freedom. Men had to stand up and decry the evils of the horrific slave trade. Someone has to stand up and decry the things that now continue to enslave the hearts of men. This is a difficult task. Maybe you are not called to do it. But you are called to live out your life as a free man. Jesus freed you. He unclasped the chains of sin from your heart and mind. Don't be a man who willingly places the harness around his own neck. Be a man who is free.

CHALLENGE: Do you believe God wants you to repeatedly fall into the same sin again and again? If you do, it's time to take steps to break the chains. Confess it to a brother. Secrets have power.

11.5 RESTORED

READ: John 21:1-25

He said to him the third time, "Simon, son of John, do you love me?" Peter was grieved because he said to him the third time, "Do you love me?" and he said to him, "Lord, you know everything; you know that I love you." Jesus said to him, "Feed my sheep. John 21:17 ESV

Peter had succumbed to his weakness. He had betrayed Jesus. He had betrayed his teacher, lord, and friend. He had betrayed someone he loved. After Peter had denied knowing Jesus he was forced to confront his weakness. I can only imagine his deep sense of sorrow and sadness. Jesus didn't want defeat to become Peter's trademark.

Jesus did know Peter loved him. Jesus had always known that Peter loved him. Jesus wanted Peter to realize it.

Your enemy will try to convince you that you are no good once you fail. Don't turn bitter. Turn to Jesus. Return to Jesus. He forgives and restores. He also trusts you to take your next step forward. Don't let the past hijack your future. Don't let echoes of your mistakes dictate your future. Go toward the purpose before you. Go with God. Go with forgiveness.

The world doesn't need men who always try to sweep their mistakes under a rug. No one needs men who refuse to acknowledge their sin. There is no place for men who always aim to refute their weakness. There is a deep need for men who know how to acknowledge their faults, pursue forgiveness, and take their next humble steps.

Imagine a world where shame has no platform, bitterness finds no fertile soil, and grace is a sign of strength. That's the world we need. That's the world you get to build when God restores what was lost inside you.

CHALLENGE: What had you given up on? What mistake did you think disqualified you? Now isn't the time to ignore it. Now is the time to make it right, seek forgiveness, and take your next step forward. Where humility and grace meet your strength is where you will shine.

DISCUSSION

What strategies do you use to resist temptation? How do you prepare yourself to avoid giving the enemy an opportune time to tempt you?

What role does selflessness play in your journey?

What lies or deceptions have you struggled with? How have you found freedom from them through Christ?

How do you ensure that you are living a life of freedom rather than becoming enslaved to vices or selfish desires?

In what ways do you stand up against the things that enslave men today? How can you encourage others to do the same?

What steps do you take to seek forgiveness and restore relationships after you've failed or made mistakes?

How does acknowledging your faults and pursuing forgiveness shape your character and leadership?

NOTES

CHAPTER 12
BE A MAN WHO LOOKS UP

"We judge of man's wisdom by his hope."

~ Ralph Waldo Emerson

12.1 THE WAY

READ: Exodus 14:1-31

*"Your way was through the sea, your path through
the great waters; yet your footprints were unseen."*
Psalm 77:19 ESV

Have you ever known a really pessimistic man? A
pessimist can suck the life out of any joyful moment.
Few men will admit they are pessimistic by nature.
This denial is usually accompanied with a cry of "I'm a
realist." Actually, you're pessimistic. You cannot be a
man who leads people toward a better tomorrow if
you're unwilling to see the potential.

The Israelites' crisis at the Red Sea is a powerful
example of this truth. Reality was stark. Of course they
couldn't lead their people across the sea. That's not
possible, at least not for men.

God will show us how to live if we pay attention.
What seems impossible is merely an opportunity.
Trust God, and follow His lead. Either what's possible
will shift or God will show you another way. But you
won't see it if you're not looking for it.

We won't know what's possible if we keep our
head down. The evidence isn't in the next step. Keep
your head high. Look up! See the goodness of God

push back the impossible before and around you. There is the way!

Never fear what seems impossible. Follow God. Trust God. Stay positive and move forward.

Your way is the direction God is leading you. Maybe God is taking you right across the sea. Perhaps God's direction for you will split the trouble in two. The evidence for what God is up to isn't found in the mud at your feet. But you can see it as He holds back the tide around you.

Be a man who looks up. Be a man of optimism. As you go toward a better tomorrow, have the faith and the courage to take your world with you.

CHALLENGE: Identify one challenging situation in your life, and take a moment today to pray and look for positive possibilities God might be leading you towards.

12.2 FOR THE GOOD

READ: Romans 8:1-39

"And we know that in all things God works for the good of those who love him, who have been called according to his purpose." Romans 8:28 NIV

Being an optimist doesn't require you to ignore reality. Optimism doesn't mean you poke your head in the dirt and pretend life never goes sideways. The man who looks up isn't ignoring the truth. He is looking for the goodness of God at work in every situation.

Scripture is filled with the stories of people encountering the goodness of God at work. Often the circumstances seemed bleak, but the goodness of God made the difference.

The man of faith trusts in his relationship with God. Having faith is the habit of believing the best about someone, and trust is the result. Trust and faith are key ingredients to optimism. Give it a shot. Besides, if you take a look around you'll see that Team Pessimist has already filled up their roster.

Guess what? Hope called. There's a spot on the team just for you. But it's hard to have hope and keep your head in the dirt. Stop filling your mind with things that drag you down. Start looking for the opportunity in difficult moments.

We have a big promise from God. We get to choose to believe it. No one can make you. But your world needs a man willing to stand in the midst of incredible hardship and look toward the horizon with hope.

The man willing to do hard things sees the obstacles in front of him as hurdles on the path rather than roadblocks in the way. They aren't detours. You can jump them and keep going. Speed up, get ready, and move forward with God—for the good of a world that needs you.

CHALLENGE: Identify an obstacle in your life you may have been avoiding. Take one simple step toward addressing it—head on.

12.3 REMAIN CONFIDENT

READ: Psalm 27:1-14

"I remain confident of this: I will see the goodness of the Lord in the land of the living. Wait for the Lord; be strong and take heart and wait for the Lord." Psalm 27:13-14 NIV

Confidence is a tricky thing. It can become a slippery slope. When we get it wrong we invest our trust in the wrong thing. We get it right, we trust the right thing. Spoiler alert—confidence in God is always the right thing.

Of course, we know this is easier said than done. Being confident you will experience goodness seems daunting when you're facing difficulty. When a loved one is diagnosed with a devastating illness, it's hard to be confident. Confidence is shaky on the day when you're laid off from work.

The key to confidence, like so many other aspects of living with your head up, is to trust God. Patience is required. Oh no! Patience? Yeah, I know. Patience is not always the strong suit for men who like to get things done. But that's often the key to confidence. Patiently wait and trust in God. Not with a weak, wobbly, pessimistic patience, but with a strong trust in God's desire to see you experience His goodness.

This becomes difficult when we confuse what God's goodness looks like. It's not measured in dollar signs and social capital. The goodness of God is what it looks like when love is blooming in your life.

Some of the most difficult moments we can experience are also the sweetest. Love is bigger, stronger, and brighter when darkness rears its ugly head. Stay confident. Be a man who knows he will see the goodness of God show up.

CHALLENGE: Pray a simple prayer today. Ask God specifically to give you confidence to trust Him in an area of difficulty you have been facing.

12.4 WITH GOD

READ: Matthew 19:1-30

Jesus looked at them and said, "With man this is impossible, but with God all things are possible."
Matthew 19:26 NIV

We have limits. There are just some things we are incapable of doing. But it can be hard to admit our limitations. Being capable of admitting our limitations is often the first step to truly acknowledging the opportunity in front of us.

The man who looks up doesn't trip over his own two feet quite as often. The man who looks up is looking for a way forward that isn't centered on his insecurity. He is a man who knows he doesn't have all the answers. He is also a man who believes there are answers to be found even in the midst of struggle.

Optimism isn't a character flaw, it is a gift. But it's one each of us must choose. Making the choice to trust God and believe He wants good things for you is the optimistic choice. Deciding you will depend on God is the optimistic choice. It's the byproduct of choosing to be a man of faith and a man willing to do hard things. Optimism doesn't always come easy.

If we made a list of things that were impossible for

us, nothing on our list would be impossible for God. He can do it all. Be a man who chooses to raise his head and look toward God when the seemingly impossible things cross his path. Model optimism in your life for those looking toward you. Examine what it looks like to lean toward an opportunity. Believe in a good outcome. Know God is with you.

It takes a bleak outlook to assume a lonely posture. That's not what God has for you. We can't predict the future. But, we can believe in a good outcome. Even more important, we can trust God will be with us no matter the outcome. What is impossible with man is possible with God.

CHALLENGE: Reexamine a recently disappointing outcome in your life. Reframe it in your mind. Would your response have been different if you'd assumed God was with you as you went through it?

12.5 REDEMPTIVE HOPE

READ: Romans 5:1-21

Not only so, but we also glory in our sufferings, because we know that suffering produces persever-ance; perseverance, character; and character, hope.
Romans 5:3-4 NIV

None of us will make it out of this alive. Scripture reminds us that we are a vapor. Our lives are a flash in the pan. That is the nature of mortality. If this was the only aspect of mortality we focused on it would hardly be an encouraging thought. Thank God it is not. For the man who looks up, it is our difficulties that tilt our head toward faith. Put another way, our hardships point us toward hope.

The man who chooses to look up will reap a harvest of hope. Make no mistake, it is a choice. The world around you is full of people who haven't embraced redemptive hope.

You are different. You know life is hard. You know you are going to face difficulties—even suffering. Don't choose to indulge in your excuses. You're not experi-encing suffering because God wants terrible things for you. Your suffering is an opportunity to develop God-given strength.

Persevere. Don't quit. Don't give up. The man who perseveres is certainly a man who will stand out in a world full of weak quitters. The man who gets back up after taking some shots is one with a character people will rally to.

Jesus suffered an excruciating death. There was nothing for him to gain. It was completely and entirely for our benefit. Hope is found in the cruelest of sufferings—the cross.

This doesn't discount your own sufferings. To write them off or attempt to belittle them is cruel. That stands completely at odds with the heart of Jesus. Jesus is the ultimate example of the man the world needs. Your suffering was never meant to be ignored.

We can identify with Jesus because of suffering. We can know hope through persistence. And, because you are a man who looks up you will be a powerful example in your world. Your world needs hope. Your world needs Jesus. And, your world needs you.

CHALLENGE: Today, choose not to speak anything negative. When someone negative shows up, choose to speak something hopeful into the situation.

DISCUSSION

How do you balance being realistic with maintaining an optimistic outlook?

In what ways have you seen God make a way for you in seemingly impossible situations? What are some practical steps you take to keep your head up and stay hopeful?

How do you build and maintain confidence in God's goodness when facing personal struggles? What role does patience play in maintaining your confidence in God?

How can you encourage others around you to adopt a more optimistic perspective? How has embracing optimism impacted your relationships and leadership?

What examples from your life demonstrate the power of looking for the good in every situation?

How can your experiences with perseverance and hope serve as a testimony to encourage others?

How do you find and focus on redemptive hope in the midst of suffering and adversity?

NOTES

AFTERWORD

NOW WHAT?

You are a man the world needs. I hope and pray you are more convinced of this truth than ever before. But, now what?

You have met together, read together, prayed, discussed, and challenged one another. What's next? What are you supposed to do with this?

Another group of men faced the same choice two thousand years ago. And, like them, a new generation of men faces this choice with each passing decade. You are a man. The world needs you. How will you choose to respond?

We can look to Jesus' brother James for a warning and a hope.

For if anyone is a hearer of the word and not a doer, he is like a man observing his natural face in a mirror; for he observes himself, goes away, and immediately forgets what kind of man he was. James 1:23-24 NIV

Don't forget what kind of man you are. You are a man the world needs. Don't let the words in this book become another set of rote platitudes that get lost in the shuffle.

Be the man God designed you to be. Be the man revealed in your heart. Be the man shaped by faith, discipline, courage, and the uncompromising Word of God. Be a man of hope, optimism, hard work, honesty and truth. Be a man people around you rally to. Be a man who leads with loving conviction and the strength of grace. Be a man the world needs.

ACKNOWLEDGMENTS

Special thanks to the amazing men of NEWBREED at New Life Church in Conway, Arkansas. You set a high bar for what it means to be a man the world needs.

I especially want to thank Ben Watson, Wayne Landers, and Jeff Strandridge for helping me sharpen these ideas. This resource wouldn't be what it has become without their friendship and insights.

I also want to give a shout out to John Sketoe and Steve Hornor. You guys are the brotherhood of encouragement. Let's climb another mountain soon.

* * *

Enjoy *Be a Man the World Needs: Volume One*?
Check out other books by Nathan King.

* * *

Everyday Jesus

Everyday Jesus: Study Guide

The Wisdom Trail Guide: 31 Steps to a Life of Wisdom

Learn Love Live: The Story God Wants For Your Life

Generational Generosity (with Richard Rogers)

The Christmas Trail Guide: 25 Days of Advent

www.ingramcontent.com/pod-product-compliance
Lightning Source LLC
LaVergne TN
LVHW051404080426
835508LV00022B/2965